Great Railway Journeys in
Europe

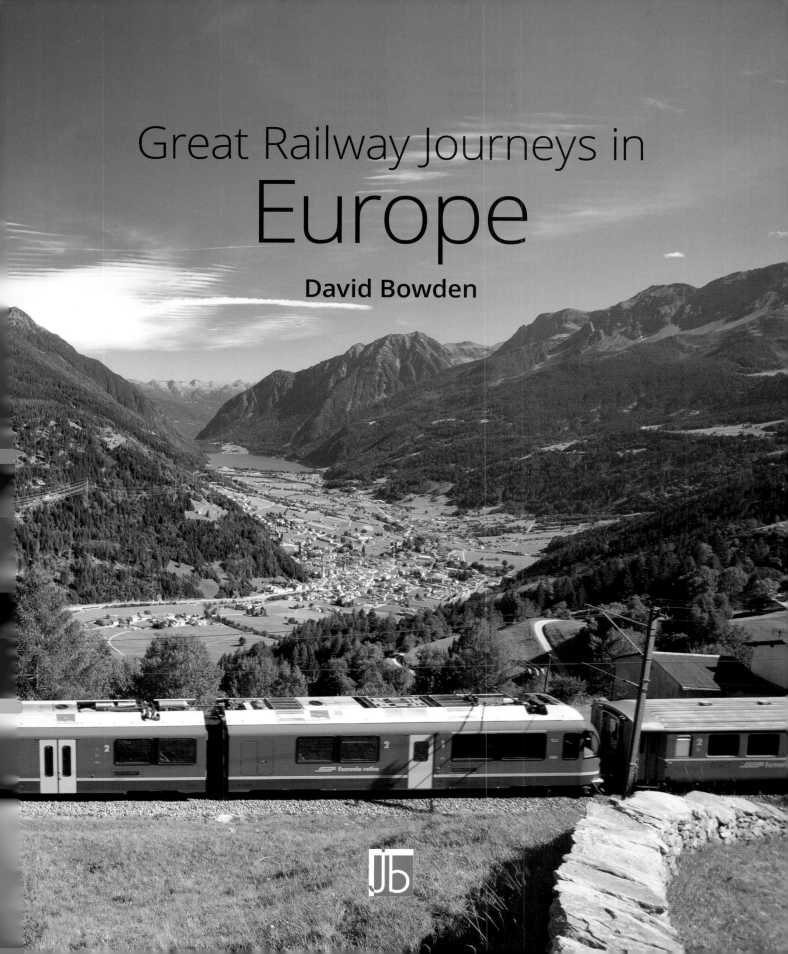

Great Railway Journeys in
Europe

David Bowden

jb

CONTENTS

Page 1 Steam trains are occasionally used on Sweden's *Inlandsbanan* line.

Pages 2–3 A train travelling above the historic town of Poschiavo on the rail line used by the *Bernina Express*.

Opposite Swiss rail operator, the Rhaetian Railway (RhB), operated the world's longest passenger train in late 2022. The train, with 100 passenger coaches extending over 1.9 km (1.2 miles), was operated by seven drivers through 22 tunnels and across 48 bridges through the Swiss Alps on the line used by the *Bernina Express*.

INTRODUCTION

There are 44 countries in Europe, and all but a few have railways. From these, a number of iconic journeys have been chosen. Some are multi-day trips in luxurious carriages, while others are short-haul excursions through picturesque scenery. The era of luxury overnight journeys lives on in some parts, but most have been replaced by high-speed trains. Budget airlines have made an impact too, as many travellers want to reach their destination as quickly as possible. However, trains do not just depart; they set off for new and enlightening experiences.

Europe would cease to function without its railways. For travellers, there are various ticket options and classes of travel, as most countries provide multi-day passes or contribute to multi-country passes such as the Eurail Pass, which can be used in 33 countries.

For convenience, European railways have been divided into the North-west, Nordic, Central and Southern regions. Railway journeys are not just about travelling from the station of embarkation to the destination, but also about the intermediary stations. Journeys have been chosen based on this, with a short description of the travel opportunities presented by each train.

NORTH-WEST EUROPE
BELGIUM

After Great Britain, Belgium was the second European country to establish a rail network. The first line, between Brussels and Mechelen, opened in 1835 and, in doing so, became the first passenger railway in continental Europe. Belgium is also acknowledged as the first European nation to establish a nationalized rail network. It was operated by the National Railway Company of Belgium (NMBS/SNCB), and the network now operates along 3,518 km (2,186 miles) of standard-gauge (1,435 mm/4 ft 8½ in) railway, of which 75 per cent is electrified.

FRANCE

The Société Nationale des Chemins de fer Français (SNCF) is the French state-owned railway company, which operates most of the passenger and freight services on the national network. France has the second-largest European rail network, with 29,900 km (18,579 miles) of track. France's first railway, from Andrézieux

to Saint-Étienne over a distance of 17 km (10.6 miles), opened in 1827. The network now extends along 29,213 km (18,152 miles) of track. Some 52 per cent is electrified, and 1,876 km (1,166 miles) is on high-speed lines – for example Trains à Grande Vitesse (TGV) high-speed trains. These were introduced in 1981 and revolutionized rail travel in France, as conventional TGV trains can operate at speeds of up to 320 km/h (200 mph). Most originate in Paris and radiate to the majority of the country. The network now covers many parts of France, but it is the Paris Métro and its suburban rail network that carries the bulk of passengers annually. France has many iconic railways, including the 'Ligne des Causses', in central southern France, the 'Swallow Railway' in the Jura Mountains, the Bergerac to Libourne route across the Purple Périgord, and the 'Yellow Train' in the Pyrénées-Orientales.

THE NETHERLANDS

The first railway in the Netherlands was built in 1839 between Amsterdam and Haarlem. Nederlandse Spoorwegen (NS) was founded in 1837, and now serves 400 destinations in the Netherlands as well as neighbouring countries. Today, the distinctive blue and yellow NS trains operate along 3,223 km (2,003 miles) of standard-gauge and mostly electrified (75 per cent) track. Double-decker carriages are a feature of the network, as is a growing network of high-speed trains.

UNITED KINGDOM

The George Stephenson-built Locomotive Number One travelled from Stockton to Darlington in north-east England on 27 September 1825. This led to the rapid global expansion of railways and tourism in general. In 1845, Thomas Cook organized the first rail excursion from Leicester to Loughborough, a distance of 19 km (12 miles). After the initial period of expansion, there was some attrition, then a general network rationalization in the 1950s and '60s, when many lines closed. However, the network remains one of the densest, busiest and largest in the world (it is the seventeenth largest). It has been growing again since the 1980s, and there has been a large programme of upgrades in recent years.

Most of the track is managed by Network Rail, which in 2017 had a network of 15,811 km (9,824 miles) of standard-gauge track

with 5,374 km (3,339 miles) electrified. In addition, most large cities have separate metro, tram and light-rail systems, while there are also numerous private railways. A number of the latter are narrow-gauge lines and primarily cater to tourists over short distances. The main rail network is connected to continental Europe via the Channel Tunnel.

NORDIC EUROPE
DENMARK

Denmark's first railway between Copenhagen and Roskilde opened in 1847. There is now 2,633 km (1,636 miles) of track, with most of it operated by the Danish State Railway (Danske Statsbaner or DSB). Arriva and Nordjyske also operate regional services in parts of the country. Denmark's first high-speed railway opened in 2019 on the Copenhagen to Ringsted Line.

FINLAND

Finland's first railway was opened in 1862 between Helsinki and Hämeenlinna. The rail network now extends along 9,216 km

Top Double-decker trains (VIRM or Verlengd InterRegio Materieel) operate as intercity services throughout the Netherlands and are the most common train type used.

Above A French TER regional train operated by SNCF passing through Pontorson, Normandy.

(5,727 miles) of 1,524 mm (5 ft) gauge track, often referred to as Russian gauge. Some 35 per cent is electrified, and passenger trains are operated by the state-owned company Yhtymä Oyj, or Finnish Rail (VR), which has services on much of the network. These services cover all big cities and towns, although the bus coverage is more extensive. Trains are modern and spacious, offering comfortable rides, and they pass through some amazing landscapes dominated by a multitude of lakes. Most lines radiate from the capital Helsinki, which also has a metro and a tram network. The Finnish trains to consider for travel are the modern tilting, Italian-built Pendolino units as well as InterCity trains. The *Santa Claus Express* from Helsinki to Rovaniemi in Lapland (page 72) is one of Europe's most exciting night trains.

NORWAY
Norway's rail network comprises 4,087 km (2,540 miles) of 1,435 mm (4 ft 8½ in) standard-gauge track. Some 64 per cent is electrified. The Norwegian Railway Directorate manages the railways on behalf of the Ministry of Transport and Communications. Various railway companies, including Vy, Flytoget, Go-Ahead and SJ Norge, operate services along these tracks. The railway from Oslo to Bergen, which is 500 km (311 miles) long, passes through lakes, forests and isolated mountain passes on Norway's

desolate Hardangervidda Plateau. This line is regarded as one of the highest mainline railways in Northern Europe. At Myrdal, the branch line to Flåm, of 20 km (12 miles), is an iconic European rail journey, passing into the picturesque mountains through spiral tunnels with steep gradients. Norway's Rauma Line is considered one of Europe's most picturesque journeys (page 64).

SWEDEN
In 1856, Sweden's first train operated along a section of the Köping to Hult Railway. The Swedish rail system is now operated by the state-owned SJ (Statens Järnvägar, or SJ AB). It uses a variety of trains, including the high-speed X2000 electric tilting trains, to all major cities. These trains normally operate at speeds of up to 200 km/h (124 mph). The network extends along 15,006 km (9,324 miles) of track, making it one of the longest in the world. Rail connections to Denmark and Norway are available, but due to rail-gauge differences, services to Finland are via bus. SJ now has competition, with companies like MTRX, Flixtrain and Snälltåget operating on select sections of the network and on to Berlin, as in the case of Snälltåget.

The multi-day *Inlandsbanan* train that travels along a remote Swedish route is one of Europe's great railway journeys (page 68).

CENTRAL EUROPE
SWITZERLAND

Switzerland has 5,223 km (3,245 miles) of track that is intricately linked to bus and boat networks (the latter including Belle Epoque paddle steamers). In 1847, the Spanisch-Brötli Line from Baden to Zürich was the first railway to operate entirely in Switzerland. Railway construction was slower than in neighbouring countries because of the mountainous terrain. The system includes 240 rail and bus companies, while Swiss Federal Railways (SBB) operates its principal railways. It has one of the world's densest public-transport networks, timed to Swiss-watchmaking precision. This network is one of the world's leading transport systems and a viable proposition for exploring Switzerland. The Grand Train Tour of Switzerland consists of a well-documented way to explore the country on eight rail routes spanning 1,280 km (795 miles), known for high quality and reliability. One of these journeys, on the GoldenPass Express, incorporates new technology that enables trains of different gauges to operate along the route from Montreux to Interlaken via Zweisimmen. A Swiss Pass is recommended for overseas visitors travelling extensively on Swiss trains. The new Gotthard Base Tunnel reduces the journey from Zürich to Milan to three and a half hours. However, speeding under the Alps through the world's longest rail tunnel in a fast train is not the best way to admire Switzerland's remarkable mountain landscape.

GERMANY

The first modern German train travelled along the Bavarian Ludwig Railway between Nuremberg and Fürth in 1835. The first long-distance railway operated between Leipzig and Dresden in 1839. The German rail network of 33,330 km (20,711 miles) is now mostly operated by the state-owned private company Deutsche Bahn (DB), with its ICE trains able to attain speeds of 300 km/h (186 mph). Some 60 per cent is electrified, and about half is double tracked. These long-distance trains serve major cities as well as neighbouring countries. Many state-subsidized regional services provide rail services to most parts of the country. DB and Australian energy company Fortescue Future Industries are working together to develop an emissions-free, ammonia-hydrogen engine as an environmentally friendly alternative to diesel engines for locomotives and rail vehicles. The Harz Railway is Europe's longest rail network that still operates daily steam trains (page 104).

AUSTRIA

Austria expanded its empire using railways. Austrian trains are now mostly operated by Österreichische Bundesbahnen (Austrian

Federal Railways, or ÖBB). ÖBB is also the administrator of Liechtenstein's railways. Its trains are known for punctuality, frequency and reliability. ÖBB operates on a track length of 4,860 km (3,020 miles), 72 per cent of which is electrified. Its bus network is equally extensive, with 50 per cent of all its passengers (330 million per annum) being bus travellers. Trains are hauled by electric and diesel locomotives, while diesel and electric railcars operate on some sectors. In 2008, high-speed or RailJet trains were introduced to operate at speeds of up to 230 km/h (143 mph). These trains are locomotive hauled, using ÖBB's existing fleet of Taurus high-speed Siemens EuroSprinter electric locomotives. RailJet is ÖBB's premier service that operates domestically and on select international routes to Germany, the Czech Republic, Italy, Switzerland, Hungary and Slovakia. ÖBB and Siemens Mobility have introduced the Viaggio Next Level of Nightjet sleeping and couchette cars. By 2025, 33 next-generation ÖBB Nightjets will provide high-speed overnight connections to several European cities. These cars were introduced in 2023 on routes from Vienna and Munich to Rome, Venice and Milan. Each seven-car Nightjet comprises two seating, three couchette and two sleeping cars with a capacity of 254 passengers. WESTbahn is a private operator serving Vienna, Salzburg, Innsbruck and Munich. It has operated since 2011 using double-decker 'KISS 3' trains manufactured in Switzerland by Stadler.

CZECH REPUBLIC

Czechoslovakia was carved from the remnants of the Austro-Hungarian Empire at the end of the First World War. Much of the railway network was built to meet the needs of the former empire, with its main routes connecting to imperial centres like Vienna, Budapest and Prague. Czech Railway (České Dráhy), extending over a network covering 9,412 km (5,484 miles), is among the best in Central Europe, and is heavily utilized by freight and passenger trains. Nádraži Praha Hlavni is Prague's main railway station.

SLOVENIA

The state railway company of Slovenia, Slovenian Railways (Slovenske železnice, or SŽ), was established in 1991. The first railway was built from Vienna to Trieste through present-day Slovenia in the 1840s (page 116). SŽ operates 1,229 km (764 miles) of standard-gauge track, with the capital Ljubljana at the heart of the network. Half the network is electrified, and there are good connections with neighbouring countries. InterCity Slovenija

(ICS) Italian-built Pendolino ETR-310 tilting trains are the finest in the fleet.

SOUTHERN EUROPE
ITALY

The first railway in Italy from Naples to Portici opened in 1839. It has an active rail network extending along 16,723 km (10,391 miles) of 1,445 mm (4 ft 8⅞ in) gauge track. Some 60 per cent is electrified. In 1939, Italian ETR 200 series trains were operating from Florence to Milan at speeds of up to 203 km/h (126 mph). This network was further expanded in the 1960s, and a new track was put in place later to enable trains to operate at 300 km/h (190 mph). The passenger train section is operated mostly by Trenitalia, with its Frecciarossa high-speed trains the finest in their fleet. Several operators use the tracks in Italy and neighbouring countries like Austria, France, Slovenia and Switzerland.

PORTUGAL

Portugal's first train departed Lisbon for Carregado in 1856. Comboios de Portugal (CP) is the state-owned railway company, which transports 145 million passengers annually. The network reached a maximum extent of 3,592 km (2,232 miles) in 1949, but later some lines were shortened or discontinued. Broad-gauge rail extends for 2,600 km (1,616 miles), with half of it electrified. The Vouga Line of just 188 km (117 miles) operates on non-electrified, metre-gauge rail. This line, inland from Aveiro on the Atlantic seaboard, is Portugal's only remaining narrow-gauge line. CP operates long-distance services, interregional, regional and urban services, as well as Lisbon and Porto's suburban trains.

International services, including night trains, extend to France and Spain. These include trains from Lisbon to Hendaye (southwest France), Lisbon to Madrid and Porto to Vigo (north-west Spain). The flagship service is the Alfa Pendular tilting train between Braga, Porto, Lisbon and Faro, which operates at speeds of up to 220 km/h (138 mph). Intercidades is a long-distance service operating to most regions at speeds of up to 200 km/h (124 mph). Inter-regional trains stop at main stations, while regional services make more stops.

Opposite A train operated by the Hungarian State Railway (MÁV) passing through the forests of Bakony Csörgö in autumn.

Portugal's planned Lisbon–Porto–Vigo High-speed Rail Project is being finalized in three phases. The first is the two-hour section between Porto and Soure, to be concluded by 2028. The second leg between Soure and Carregado is planned for a 2030 completion with a time of 79 minutes. The third phase, between Carregado and Lisbon, will be built later to enable a final journey time of 75 minutes between Porto and Lisbon.

SPAIN

The first railway on the Iberian Peninsula opened in 1848, from Barcelona to Mataró. Renfe (Red Nacional de los Ferrocarriles Españoles) is the state-owned railway that operates most services in Spain. Its network of 16,026 km (10,182 miles), of which 64 per cent is electrified, includes 1,668 mm (5 ft 5 21⁄32 in) gauge, 1,435 mm (4 ft 8½ in) standard gauge, and the 1,000 mm (3 ft 3⅜ in) metre gauge. In 2005, the old Renfe national company was split into ADIF (infrastructure) and Renfe-Operadora (rolling stock). The railway has just expanded its network with some 100 new trains, including high-capacity suburban EMUs manufactured by Stadler and Alstom, and 30 medium-distance trains. Several luxurious, multi-day rail excursions are also available in Spain (page 142).

GREECE

Greece has 5,256 km (3,266 miles) of track with 30 per cent electrified. Its main track is 1,435 mm (4 ft 8½ in) standard gauge, while there are other lines of various narrow gauges. The first railway completed was the Athens to Piraeus Railway in 1869. The network reached its peak in 1940, but then routes began to be eliminated and shortened, and services cut. The remaining services, operated by Hellenic Train and some private companies, are being slowly modernized. The fully electrified Piraeus to Platy via Athens line is Greece's busiest passenger route.

EASTERN EUROPE & THE BALKANS
BOSNIA & HERZEGOVINA

Until independence in 1992, the rail network of 1,031 km (641 miles) was part of Yugoslav Railways. The Balkan state of Bosnia and Herzegovina has two political-territorial divisions that include the Republic of Srpska. Its rail network is operated by the Railways of the Federation of Bosnia and Herzegovina (ŽFBH) and Željeznice Republike Srpske (ŽRS) in Srpska. The former operates 608 km (378 miles) of track, with the latter operating 424 km (263 miles). The networks are being upgraded and are now able to accommodate modern Spanish-built TALGO trains.

ROMANIA

Romania's first railway opened in 1854, and in 1880 the current operator, Căile Ferate Române (CFR), was established. It operates 10,777 km (6,697 miles) of track with some 37 per cent being electrified. Its lines provide rail interconnectivity with all its European neighbours.

BULGARIA

The Bulgarian State Railways (BDŽ) is the country's state railway company, with its headquarters in the capital Sofia. It oversees (2,485 miles) of 1,435 mm (4 ft 7 in) track, and the 760 mm (2 ft 5 in) narrow-gauge Septemvri to Dobrinishte route (page 154).

HUNGARY

Hungarian State Railways (MÁV) operates the national railway, with MÁV-Start being responsible for passenger transport. The nation's first railway, from Pest to Vác, opened in 1846. By 1910, the Hungarian rail network was one of Europe's biggest, covering 22,869 km (14,210 miles). It connected 1,490 stations, making it one of the densest railways in the world. It has declined to 7,606 km (4,726 miles) of primarily standard gauge, but with some broad- and narrow-gauge lines. Plans are in place for 50 new

Siemens Vectron locomotives and 39 train sets to join the current fleet. A unique railway is the Budapest Children's Railway, built in 1948. It operates through the forests of Buda between Hűvösvölgy and Széchenyi-Hill. Apart from driving the locomotive, children control the railway.

POLAND

Polskie Koleje Państwowe (Polish State Railway, or PKP) is the state-owned enterprise and the dominant operator of trains in Poland. The network of 18,510 km (11,500 miles) operates on a 1,435 mm (4 ft 8½ in) gauge track from Warsaw (Warszawa) to major domestic destinations like Kraków, Gdańsk, Katowice and Poznań. International services extend to destinations like Berlin, Prague and Vilnius. New national and international open-access services have been announced on the Kraków–Częstochowa, Przemyśl–Medyka, Prague–Gdańsk, Prague–Kraków and Kraków–Warsaw routes. These services will be provided by Polish operator Koleje Małopolskie, five by Czech operator RegioJet, and one by Czech operator Leo Express.

Spain's network of Alta Velocidad Española (AVE) trains is the most extensive of any European country and is globally only surpassed by China.

NORTH-WEST EUROPE
PARIS TO ISTANBUL ON THE *ORIENT EXPRESS*

THE ART OF LUXURY TRAVEL

The *Venice Simplon-Orient-Express* is one of the world's most famous trains, if not its most legendary. In his book *Ghost Train to the Eastern Star*, author Paul Theroux wrote that the *Orient Express* enjoys success with the nostalgic rich. Now operated by Belmond, the train has become the world's most famous set of carriages, and on its various multi-day journeys, passengers experience them at their elegant best. With its polished wood, sumptuous upholstery and antique fixtures, the train epitomizes the elegance and glamour of a golden era of rail travel.

The train's fame is possibly attributed to another author, Agatha Christie, whose novel *Murder on the Orient Express* ensured its notoriety and made it an aspirational journey for many travellers. This is all despite the fact that the train in its purest form has not operated for decades.

Christie's best-selling novel created a certain mystique and suspense, while geopolitical changes along the route through the decades have added to the train's notoriety. Luxurious tour trains operated by the Moët Hennessy Louis Vuitton (LVMH)-owned Belmond travel brand have adopted the train's name and offer elements of classic styling from the grand era of train travel.

The original *Venice Simplon-Orient-Express* was a train service that operated on several different European routes. In its original incarnation, it was a rail service that ran from Paris to Istanbul and connected to Vienna and Budapest along the way.

Another misconception is the use of the term 'Orient'. To

Opposite Posters promoting travel on the Paris-Vienne-Constantinople route have been used to attract travellers onto the *Orient Express* from its beginning in 1882.

Left The *Orient Express* has promised luxurious rail travel for discerning travellers since its inception.

Right The Piano Bar is popular with passengers, who dress up each evening to share their travel adventures.

travellers in the Victorian era, the 'Orient' had a very different meaning than it has today. While the train operated eastwards from Paris, the Orient inferred countries to the 'east' of Western Europe. In Roman times, the Eastern Empire included 'Orient' in its description and referred essentially to the Balkans.

Constantinople (now Istanbul) on the Bosphorus Strait was the official demarcation between Europe on the waterway's western shores and Asia on its eastern shore. Now very much one urban area separated by water, the city was considered the gateway to Asia and the seat of the powerful Ottoman Empire.

The Turkish Straits link the Black Sea to the Sea of Marmara and separate European Turkey from Asian Turkey along what is known as the Bosphorus. Haydarpasa Station on the Asian side of Istanbul has been described as a dark, heavy European building and an incongruous gateway to Asia. It was built in 1909 based on drawings made by a German architect. Trains head east towards Ankara, the capital of Turkey (now Türkiye), and across Central Asia.

Today, 'Orient' tends to mean the Far East, which was beyond the horizon as far as late-nineteenth-century railway travellers from Paris were concerned.

Interestingly, Belmond also operates the *Eastern and Oriental Express*, which has a somewhat superfluous name, as 'eastern' and 'Oriental' are interchangeable. The suggestion that this train is an express is also misleading, as the journey is anything but fast, with the train covering some 1,920 km (1,233 miles) on its four-day, three-night journey from Bangkok to Singapore.

TRACK NOTES

In 1882, Georges Nagelmackers, an engineer and son of a Belgian banker, invited guests on a return rail journey of 2,000 km (1,243 miles) on his *Train Eclair de luxe* (lightning luxury test train). They departed on 10 October 1882 from Paris Gare de l'Est for Vienna. The journey to Vienna took just under 30 hours before it returned to Paris. The tradition of fine dining began on the very first journey, with Nagelmackers's guests dining on oysters, soup with Italian pasta, turbot with green sauce, chicken *à la chasseur*, fillet of beef with *château* potatoes, *chaud-froid* sauce of game animals, lettuce, chocolate pudding and a buffet of desserts.

The service became a commercial proposition in 1883, and other services were added to other European cities. On these, the journey was as important as the destination, with modern-day travellers venturing on these luxury trains for the experience rather than simply to arrive at another European destination.

When Nagelmackers conceived the idea, there was a lack of integration between the railways of Europe that made continental travel difficult and arduous. His solution involved the provision of sleeping cars known as wagons-lits. He was inspired by travelling in Pullman sleeping-car carriages in the United States.

Nagelmackers's Compagnie Internationale des Wagons-Lits offered cross-border travel with a degree of luxury. The service simplified travel between countries, especially for wealthy travellers with lots of luggage. He combined the concept of steamship convenience and comfort with the speed and service of the railway. Over the years, Wagons-Lits expanded greatly across Europe and operated a host of deluxe international services, of which *Orient Express* remained one of the best known.

The exotic imagery conveyed by travelling from Paris to the east was very compelling, so much so that it continued to sell Wagons-Lits' *Orient Express* for decades. For the purist, the true *Orient Express* died with the onset of the First World War, yet the train, in name and in spirit, was revised and adjusted several times over the years. After the war, the *Simplon-Orient-Express* was introduced on a southerly route through France, Switzerland, northern Italy and the recently created Yugoslavia. It avoided Germany and Austria altogether, and took advantage of the 20 km (12 mile) Simplon Tunnel from Switzerland through to Italy that opened in 1906 (a second parallel tunnel opened in 1921). This train followed a completely new route, and took in Milan, Venice, Trieste, Zagreb and Belgrade before continuing to Istanbul. Constantinople was renamed Istanbul when Turkey was established in 1922.

During the 1920s, the rebuilding of German and Austrian lines allowed Wagons-Lits to resume a more traditional *Orient Express* routing, as well as a trans-alpine service over the Arlberg Pass in Austria called the *Arlberg-Orient Express*, which began in 1932. The Second World War caused Wagons-Lits to suspend service for a number of years. By the 1960s, Cold War tensions effectively truncated the train at Vienna, eliminating the most exotic portion of the journey. Although it carried the *Orient Express* name, the train appeared little different from most other European intercity express trains.

In the 1970s, American businessman James Sherwood, Belmond's founder, bought several dilapidated carriages at an auction and ploughed millions into restoring them for their 1982 re-entry to service. The name *Orient Express* survived into the mid-2000s, but it had none of the panache of its historic antecedent.

WELCOME ABOARD

The Belmond *Venice Simplon-Orient-Express* comprises 11 sleeping cars, three restaurant cars, one bar car and two staff cars, making it Europe's longest passenger train. Each of the 17 carriages was once part of Europe's iconic *Orient Express*, a timeless heritage train service that once connected Paris to Istanbul.

Most of the carriages are from the interwar period (the oldest dates back to 1926) and are painted in the traditional cream and navy, with wonderfully restored interiors, opulently finished in plush fabric, varnished wooden panels and polished metal fixtures.

In mid-2023, Belmond unveiled a new cabin category aboard the legendary *Venice Simplon-Orient-Express*. Joining the two pre-existing cabin categories, the new suites provide further opulence on the train. French artisans and designers who reimagined these suites retained elements of the golden era of travel in the 1920s and '30s, while incorporating contemporary facilities and comfort in two of the original carriages. The historic cabins on the train have the same timelessness, and are transformed from daytime lounges into comfortable lower and upper berth beds each evening.

The new suites celebrate the dramatic landscape that unfolds along the train's journey. The four different designs are: La Campagne (the countryside), Les Montagnes (the mountains), Les Lacs (the lakes), and La Forêt (the forest). La Campagne is a tribute to the vineyards of northern Italy and the Côte d'Azur of southern France. La Forêt-inspired suites reflect the Black Forest in Germany's mountainous south-west, a route taken when the train travels from Prague to Paris. Austria's Arlberg massif is witnessed on the train's classic route to Venice, with Les Montagnes suites making reference to these mountainous peaks. The Les Lacs motif reflects the beauty of many spectacular lakes passed en route, from Zurgersee in Switzerland to Lake Como in Italy.

Each suite is adorned with plush Art Deco fabrics and furnishings. All suites include a private marble en-suite bathroom with shower, as well as a lounge area by day, converted to either double or twin beds by night. Private dining is possible, with the

Opposite Small villages such as Roppen provide a window on picturesque rural life as the train heads towards Innsbruck in the Austrian Tyrol.

Below The train passes through Switzerland's dramatic scenery on its alpine journey to Italy along an historic route between northern and southern Europe.

lounge set up on a 24-hour cabin-service basis that is inclusive of free-flowing Champagne.

ATTENTION TO DETAIL

Various Belmond *Venice Simplon-Orient-Express* trains travel through Europe: Czech Republic (Prague), France (Paris and Cannes), Italy (Florence, Venice, Rome and Verona), Austria (Vienna and Innsbruck), Hungary (Budapest), Romania (Bucharest), Switzerland (Geneva), Belgium (Brussels) and the Netherlands (Amsterdam). These journeys are made from March to November. The iconic Paris to Istanbul route operates just once a year.

The London–Paris–Venice, Pullman-style train is a two-day, one-night journey. The route requires two sets of equipment, which has historical precedents. Passengers board a restored British Pullman train at London's Victoria Station and travel to Kent, where they transfer to a ferry. On arriving on the Continent, they board another luxury train, equipped for the overnight journey to Italy. Typically, Belmond trains operate from Calais, France, southwards via the Gare de l'Est in Paris, then east through Switzerland and south to Verona, Italy, before pulling into Venice. While both directions offer a wonderful experience, most travellers prefer the southbound run. An alternate routing boards at Bruges, Belgium and operates via Germany. Belmond also offers what it calls a 'Signature Journey' that more closely follows the route of Nagelmackers's 1883 inaugural train. It travels from Paris to Budapest and Istanbul. This is a six-day, five-night journey that may only operate once a year. The train's history, mystique and opulence cntinue to appeal to aspirational travellers.

France's Compagnie de l'Est operated the original train to Alsace-Lorraine, which was then part of Germany. It continued on various German state railways via Karlsruhe and Stuttgart, up the Geislingen incline, and across Bavaria to München (Munich). Once in the Hapsburg domains, it travelled via Salzburg, Vienna and Budapest. East of Budapest the route changed a number of times as improved means of reaching the Bosphorus were devised.

Although it has been many years since travellers could board a scheduled passenger train at Gare de l'Est with a direct run to Istanbul, it is still possible to travel this route via scheduled first-class services while experiencing the overnight portions in a sleeping car. Although passengers have to change trains, the service is much quicker than in Victorian times. At its inception, the original route required a 75-hour journey (and that was considered

Right Passengers on the *Venice Simplon-Orient-Express* can travel in luxuriously appointed cabins such as the Grand Suite.

vastly quicker than earlier options). Today, with train changes, travellers can make the trip in just 58 hours.

Begin on a Sunday, having enjoyed a full day in Paris exploring the city's alluring sights, which could include a visit to the Louvre on the right bank of the River Seine. For those who like to blend railway interest with art appreciation, a visit to the Museé d'Orsay is interesting as the building was once Gare d'Orsay, a main station on the Paris to Orléans line. Other possibilities include a visit to the Eiffel Tower, or a journey on the RER suburban lines to Louis XIV's Palace at Versailles. Take time to dine in Paris before boarding, as there is no formal diner on the train, although snacks and light meals are available.

Trains to the east begin at Gare de l'Est, one of Paris' six main railway terminals. It is adjacent to Gare du Nord (the terminus for the Eurostar and Thalys high-speed trains). Pre-booked reservations for the City Night Line 'hotel train' to Munich are mandatory. The train departs platform 13 at 8 p.m. sharp and runs overnight to the Bavarian capital, following much of the same route as the old *Orient Express*.

The tracks and equipment have been much improved since Georges Nagelmackers's original train, and passengers now glide along in modern comfort, if not Victorian opulence. Overnight the train crosses the German frontier and travels via one of the steepest main lines in Germany east of Stuttgart, the famed Geislingen incline (1 in 44.5), and beyond via the historic city of Ulm. The days of pausing for a steam banking engine to assist

have long since passed, and today the route is completely electrified.

Passengers arrive at the busy München Hauptbahnhof (Munich Railway Station) just after 7 a.m. and have a leisurely two and a half hours to change trains, allowing them to take the time to have breakfast in one of the station restaurants. Just before 9.30 a.m., the RailJet (RJ63) for Budapest via Salzburg and Vienna departs. This is a fine train and the scenery is splendid. On the way to Wien (Vienna) the train follows the Danube valley. While portions of the original line are used, modern upgrades have straightened the Austrian Westbahn into a modern transportation route. The run between Vienna and Budapest follows a traditional route.

The RailJet serves Budapest Keleti (East Station), the most interesting of the Hungarian capital's main railway terminals, featuring a vast train shed with a characteristic fan-shaped front window. This was a traditional stop for the *Orient Express* and still conveys a feeling of adventurous travel. The differences between Western and Eastern Europe become readily apparent on the journey to the east.

At Budapest passengers change to a EuroNight train (EN473), which departs just after 7 p.m. This has more in common with traditional overnight trains of the mid-twentieth century than the overly sanitized City Night Line. However, Hungarian first-class trains are generally of a high standard and this one is scheduled to carry a restaurant car, so plan for dinner on the train. The journey over the Hungarian plains east of Budapest is conducted in darkness, but the journey over the Transylvanian Alps (otherwise known as the Southern Carpathians), is done in daylight. The territory is famous as the birthplace of Vlad Tepes, the vicious medieval lord who inspired Bram Stoker's Dracula. Some passengers may want to take an imaginary trip following the trail of Stoker's Jonathan Harker on his journey from London to meet Count Dracula (the story begins with Harker's train ride.)

At Bucuresti Nord (Bucharest North Station) travellers face a tight connection with a Romanian fast train that includes sleepers to Istanbul. Only 20 minutes are allowed, and depending on the timeliness of the train from Budapest, the wise traveller wastes no time in changing from one to the other.

Travellers depart Bucharest at 12.30 p.m. and travel via Bulgaria and western Turkey for arrival at Istanbul Sirkeci just before 8 a.m. the next morning. Having departed Paris on a Sunday night, adventurous travellers will have arrived on a Wednesday morning and will have had a journey through seven nations. Although no longer an opulent through run, this remains one of the world's great railway journeys.

THE TRAIN AS A MURDER MYSTERY

Without a doubt, the acclaimed 1934 novel *Murder on the Orient Express* (first published in the United States in 1934 as *Murder on the Calais Express*), by Dame Agatha Christie, has inspired countless travellers to add the train journey from Paris to Istanbul to their travel wish lists. The complex plot is unravelled by Hercule Poirot, a compulsive obsessive Belgian detective who happens to be travelling on the train when American businessman Samuel Ratchett is murdered in an adjoining sleeping berth.

The novel has also been celebrated in various film, radio and television versions, including a 1974 British-made film, a 2001 and 2010 television series.

While Christie's novel commences in Istanbul, the bulk of it unfolds in what was then Yugoslavia, with the train trapped in a snowdrift between Vinkovci and Brod (now eastern Croatia). There is a suggestion that Christie received inspiration for the novel while delayed for a day during her journey on the train in March 1932. Also, Christie's plot involves a kidnapping that appears to be based on the snatching and murder of Charles Lindbergh Junior in the United States, which garnered global attention in 1932.

It has been reported that the original film and one of another Agatha Christie's mystery novels were the only two book-to-film adaptations that the author liked. She attended the London premiere of the 1974 film, but died just 14 months afterwards.

Below A Deutsche Bahn (DB) at the top of the Geislingen incline on the German section of the route.

EUROSTAR

BRITAIN'S RAIL LINK TO THE CONTINENT

The ability to board a high-speed train in London and travel to various continental capitals in just over two hours is one of history's greatest railway achievements. Highlights of the Eurostar journey include departing from London to several European terminals in a modern train and travelling at speeds of 300 km/h (186 mph) in comfort and safety while zipping below the English Channel. This allows for a fast journey from London to Paris's Gare du Nord, which is more competitive than flying. The fastest Eurostar over the route of 492 km (305 miles) covers the non-stop journey in 135 minutes.

Britain's proximity to continental Europe and the constant necessity of crossing the English Channel by boat encouraged generations of engineers and planners to dream of building a tunnel to connect England with France. French engineer Albert Mathieu first proposed the construction of a trans-channel tunnel in 1800, a generation before the world's first public steam railway came into service. Up until the 1990s, passengers bound for the Continent needed to take a ferry across the English Channel to reach France.

Over the years, numerous plans for channel tunnels and bridges were discussed, and tunnel companies were formed. In the 1980s, a serious plan began, and in May 1994 the tunnel was opened by the late Queen Elizabeth II and French President François Mitterrand. International high-speed Eurostar services began at the end of that year.

The opening of the Channel Tunnel (Chunnel) enabled direct rail connections between London and the Continent. While France's high-speed link to the Channel Tunnel was ready in time for the tunnel's opening, Britain took another 14 years to complete its connections. Initially, Eurostar trains began their journey from an international terminal at Waterloo Station, with trains operating to Paris and Brussels, plus seasonal services to the Swiss Alps. In 2008, the transformed and fully modernized St Pancras Station opened as London's new international terminal. This enabled Eurostar services to operate from the magnificent, 1867-built, balloon-style iron train shed.

Today, the Channel Tunnel is one of Europe's most important sections of the Continent's railway infrastructure. It is 50.5 km (31.4 miles) long, of which 38.6 km (24 miles) are located 45 m

(147.6 ft) below the English Channel between Britain and Europe. This makes it the longest underwater tunnel in the world.

Eurostar was established in 1994 as a partnership between three railway companies: SNCF (France), SNCB (Belgium) and LCR (London and Continental Railways). The United Kingdom government disposed of its share to private equity holders in 2015, and in 2023, Eurostar and Belgian railway operator Thalys came under the same management.

TRACK NOTES

Eurostar, the international high-speed passenger rail service, links Britain with several city-centre stations in mainland Europe. It offers one of Europe's great rail journeys, with its two main continental stations being Paris Gare du Nord and Brussels Bruxelles-Midi Station. There are currently another 12 destinations, including Calais, Lille, Amsterdam, Rotterdam, Lyon, Avignon and Marseille, three French skiing destinations (Moutiers, Aime-La-Plage and Bourg-Saint-Maurice), and Marne-la-Vallée-Chessy (Disneyland Paris).

Eurostar trains are an adaptation of the French TGV design. Not only do trains travel at high speeds, but they also need to operate using a variety of different electrification systems and to comply with the signalling requirements of each country.

The service uses specially built high-speed lines that pass through the world-famous English Channel. The tunnel is made of three parallel tubes: two outside bores each carrying a single railway track, while a narrower central bore is a service tunnel.

The current Eurostar train, first introduced into service in 1994, can carry 750 passengers at operating speeds of up to 300 km/h (186 mph) but the e320 train, introduced in 2015, can carry up to 900 passengers at speeds of up to 320 km/h (199 mph). There are 28 train sets in the current Eurostar fleet, including 11 Class 373/1 trains, each with 18 coaches, and 17 Class 374 trains, each with 16 coaches.

Top The entrance to the station adjoins St Pancras Renaissance London Hotel with the hotel entrance often confused by passengers departing London for Europe on Eurostar trains.

Above Eurostar has plans to carry 30 million passengers annually on its current fleet of 51 trains all branded with an iconic star as their symbol and new logo.

Right Eurostar services from London and Amsterdam call into Rotterdam Centraal Station with, its striking stainless steel roof.

Opposite Eurostar services terminate or originate from Amsterdam's Centraal Station, which was designed by Petrus Cuypes, best known for the nearby Rijksmuseum, which houses Rembrandt's famous painting, 'The Night Watch'.

WELCOME ABOARD

Passengers begin their journey in London in the magnificently transformed St Pancras International Terminal at King's Cross. The adjoining St Pancras Renaissance London Hotel confuses many passengers, who think it is part of the station. The former Grand Midland Hotel, built in 1873, is now managed by Marriott and integrated into the multi-tier transportation hub. It has been featured in numerous films, including two *Harry Potter* films, which explains why the retail shop and photo opportunity the Harry Potter Shop at Platform 9¾, is located at the station.

Customers travelling on Eurostar can enjoy a range of benefits, including boarding at downtown city-centre stations, sitting in comfortable seats that have spacious leg room, with complimentary Wi-Fi connectivity, in-seat power sockets and onboard entertainment. Passengers are allowed to carry two suitcases and one piece of hand luggage on board. Luggage racks are located at either end of each carriage and it is best to arrive early to secure a space.

With Britain's withdrawal from the European Union,

immigration and customs checks are now part of the travel experience, and Eurostar management suggests arriving between 90 and 120 minutes before departure, which defeats one of the train's advantages over flying (45 to 60 minutes is the suggested time for passengers travelling in the two premium classes). However, as travellers become more conscious of their carbon footprint, the operators of Eurostar and many other trains in Europe promote the environmental benefits of high-speed rail in releasing fewer carbon emissions into the atmosphere than aircraft over similar distances.

There are three types of seating available on each service – Standard, Standard Premium and Business Premium Class. The seating in Standard Class is two by two with a centre aisle; in the Premium Classes the seating is one by two with a centre aisle. Passengers travelling in the Business Premium Service are offered flexible fares up to departure, express check-in, and exclusive access to business lounges in London and Paris, as well as complimentary drinks and fine seasonal dining designed by Michelin-starred chefs in the lounge and in the comfort of their seats. Many cocktails are made with Eurostar's own gin, Toujours 21.

Passengers travelling in the somewhat unusually named Standard Premium Class are served a snack (a choice between two dishes) and a beverage (alcoholic or non-alcoholic) at their seat, but do not have access to the lounge before travelling.

While trains do not provide a dining car, Eurostar offers Café Métropole, a kiosk that sells hot and cold drinks, snacks and meals, as well as a range of alcoholic beverages.

ATTENTION TO DETAIL

Eurostar runs from London's St Pancras Station to Gare du Nord in Paris every hour or so, seven days a week. The other possible British stops are Ebbsfleet International and Ashford International in Kent. Some trains in France may stop at Calais-Fréthun and Lille-Europe. Trains to Belgium and the Netherlands serve Brussels-South and Rotterdam Central (Centraal), before arriving at the Amsterdam Central (Centraal) terminal. There are also direct services from London to Marne-la-Vallée–Chessy (Disneyland Paris) a few times per week and seasonal direct services to the French Alps during the winter skiing season. However, the future of the Disneyland service is in doubt.

The Eurostar service from London to Rotterdam and Amsterdam is relatively new. This now means that a transfer to Brussels is no longer a necessity. On its journey from London, the train stops at

Rotterdam Central before arriving at Amsterdam Central just three and a half hours later. Passengers must now complete passport and customs procedures when they first alight in Europe. Belgian and French sections of the network are shared with Thalys services and TGV trains running between Paris and Brussels.

Over the years, fares have dropped in an effort to compete with low-cost air carriers. This does not affect children under four years of age, who travel for free.

There are currently 15 daily departures during weekdays from London to Paris, although there are more on Fridays. Most are non-stop. The London to Brussels route is served by nine weekday trains, while there is only one service from London to Amsterdam via Brussels, Lille and Rotterdam.

The expansion of European high-speed railway networks and the opening of the Channel Tunnel have made it easier to travel by train between Britain and mainland Europe.

DERRY TO COLERAINE
A MOST BEAUTIFUL RAILWAY JOURNEY

While some debate the use of Derry or Londonderry, few would argue with Michael Palin, who described the rail route from this Northern Ireland destination to nearby Coleraine as 'one of the most beautiful railway journeys in the world'. The line between Coleraine and Derry operated by Translink NI Railways (Northern Ireland Railways, or NIR) has recently undergone a phased upgrade programme. This section of track is part of the line to Belfast and of the 357 km (222 miles) of 1,600 mm (5 ft 3 in) gauge track operated by NIR.

The line in County Londonderry was built by the Londonderry and Coleraine Railway Company (L&CR) in 1845–1853. The route began at Derry, on the eastern bank of the Foyle River. In 1852, the first section of the railway between Londonderry and Limavady opened, mostly for freight. The line through to Coleraine was fully completed in July 1853, eight years after the project began. Not long after, the line was absorbed into the Belfast and Northern Counties Railway.

Initially, the line terminated on the west bank of the River Bann, but in late 1860, a viaduct across the river opened to enable Derry trains to head all the way to Belfast. In 1855, a roughly north–south line from Ballymena to Portrush via Coleraine opened.

As well as the main line between Londonderry and Coleraine, branch lines once operated. There was a ferry service between Magilligan and Magilligan Point at the mouth of Lough Foyle. It only operated for a short time and closed late in 1855, making it Ireland's briefest passenger line.

While the Londonderry to Limavady section opened in 1852, work towards Coleraine started west of Limavady Station. Thus, Limavady became a branch line that was extended inland to Dungiven by 1883. This operated as the Limavady and Dungiven Railway from the mid-nineteenth century until 1950 for passengers, and 1955 for freight.

In 2016, the late Queen Elizabeth II took a steam-hauled train from Coleraine to Bellarena to recreate a small section of a trip she made just a month after her coronation in 1953.

The line is highly regarded for its panoramic coastal scenery, especially along Downhill Beach, the Binevenagh mountainside and the River Foyle estuary.

TRACK NOTES
While diesel cars were introduced in the 1950s, steam locomotives continued on the mostly single-track line until the end of the 1960s. In 2005, the first of NIR's 3000 Class DMUs were introduced on the service with an operational speed of up to 145 km/h (90 mph). Similar in appearance, the Class 4000 DMUs, introduced in 2011, have more powerful engines. They also have less seating and just one toilet as opposed to two on the 3000 DMUs. Both are three-car units, but additional carriages were purchased to convert some to six-car trains. Upholstered seating, fold-down tables, Wi-Fi, USB ports and wheelchair access are all provided.

WELCOME ABOARD
Trains depart from Derry Station, which is now the North-West Transport Hub. This is the old Derry Waterside Station, which ceased operations in the 1980s after two bomb attacks. Derry is a vibrant city with a long history, including the seventeenth-century

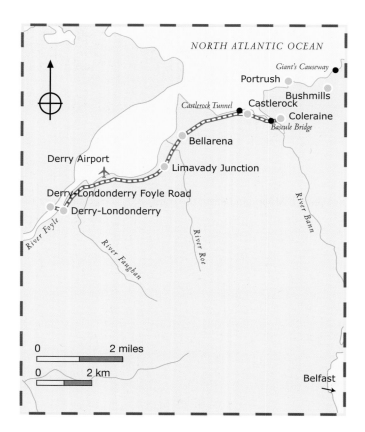

Trains operated by Translink travel past Downhill, one of the most scenic sections of the Derry to Coleraine line.

Derry's Walls. Passengers can use the free connecting bus from the city to the train station or walk across the River Foyle via the Peace Bridge. Departing trains soon pass St Columb's Park and head beyond the city limits. The track grips the eastern shore of the River Foyle and passes beneath the Foyle Bridge and the A515 Motorway, heading westwards to the border with Ireland.

There are only four remaining stations on the line – Derry, Bellarena, Castlerock and Coleraine. Many stations, some of which were just basic platforms, came and went over time. Some of the former station buildings have been converted into private residences. Passengers can alight at Bellarena and Castlerock and rejoin a later train.

The original Bellarena Station, designed by John Lanyon and built between 1873 and 1875, is now a private residence. It closed in 1976 and reopened in 1982. The new station was erected in 2016, and has twin platforms and a passing loop that was opened by Queen Elizabeth II in 2019.

As the train passes close to the beachfront of Downhill, passengers can admire Benone Strand, cliffs, Dunne Waterfall and Binevenagh Mountain before the train enters two tunnels on its journey eastwards along the coast towards Castlerock. The line first enters the Downhill Tunnel of 275 m (902 ft), and briefly travels in the open before entering the Castlerock Tunnel of 611 m (2,005 ft). The latter is Ireland's longest railway tunnel. Work began in 1846 on this major engineering feat, with blasting completed one year later.

In 2002, a landslide at Downhill caused boulders to crash on to the line, resulting in a derailment. Netting was installed along the cliffs and can be seen from the train. Castlerock Station was erected in 1874, and its signal box, which was closed in 2016, was the last in Northern Ireland to use mechanical signals and tokens.

The small, circular Mussenden Temple is situated above Downhill Tunnel. Built in 1785, the building was erected as a library modelled on Rome's Temple of Vesta in the Forum Romanum.

Castlerock is a popular seaside village that has seen a surge in popularity since Downhill Beach was used as a backdrop in *Game of Thrones*. Its beaches are frequented in summer, and accommodation is provided in flats and caravan parks.

ATTENTION TO DETAIL

The route is operated by government-owned Translink NI Railways, and it forms part of the Belfast to Londonderry service. Once threatened with closure, an all-island strategic rail review is currently assessing rail connectivity, especially in this part of Northern Ireland.

Passengers can join the train at one of the four stops on the route or at platform four of Belfast Lanyon Place for the service to Coleraine. The train from Belfast makes a few stops before arriving at Coleraine, then continuing on to Derry. This journey takes a little over two hours to complete, while that from Coleraine to Derry takes just 50 minutes. There are some 16 services per day, mostly an hour apart, with the first departing Derry at 6.12 a.m. and the last at 9.38 p.m. The first train from Coleraine to Derry departs at 7.43 a.m. and the last at 10.43 p.m. Weekend services are slightly different. Discounted tickets are available for travel outside peak hours.

Passengers who sit on the left-hand side of the train to Coleraine, and the right-hand side for Derry, will get the most enjoyment from the coastal scenery. However, inclement weather will affect the full impact of the coastal scenery.

Additional extensions for train enthusiasts around Coleraine are the line of 8 km (5 miles) to Portrush, the Giant's Causeway and Bushmills Railway. Regular services depart from Coleraine for Portrush and take just 12 minutes travelling via the University of Ulster campus.

The former Derry Railway Station, built in 1873, has been restored and repurposed as the North-West Transport Hub.

GIANT'S CAUSEWAY & BUSHMILLS RAILWAY

The Giant's Causeway & Bushmills Railway (GC&BR) is a 914 mm (3 ft) narrow-gauge heritage railway operating between Bushmills and the Giant's Causeway on the coast to the north-east of Coleraine. The existing line is just 3.2 km (2 miles) long, but it originally extended all the way to Portrush. When the original line opened, it was heralded as the world's first long electric tramway, as it was powered by hydroelectricity provided from an elevated third rail. Initially, steam tram engines were also used, but in 1899 the power was supplied from overhead wires. The line to Bushmills opened in 1883, and the extension to the Giant Causeway opened in 1887. It closed in 1949 and was dismantled.

A new tourist service was conceived and opened in 2002. It now operates customized four-coach diesel multiple units (DMU) that can carry up to 90 passengers. The service attempts to recreate the original hydroelectric tram experience. The new DMU is powered by a Kubota V3600-E3 engine, and it travels alongside the existing fleet of steam locomotives. Trains depart from just west of Bushmills village and travel northwards through the Bushfoot Golf Course, across the Bushfoot River, and close to Bushfoot Beach, before terminating at Causeway Head. From here, the UNESCO-recognized Giant's Causeway basalt formations are a short walk away. Bushmills is also home to the Bushmills Distillery, the world's oldest licensed whisky distillery, which provides tours for connoisseurs to admire its blended and single malt whiskys aged up to 21 years. Bus services 402, 172 and 177 connect Coleraine to Bushmills and the Giant's Causeway via Dunluce Castle and the scenic Causeway Coastal Route.

CALEDONIAN SLEEPER

OVERNIGHT TO THE SCOTTISH HIGHLANDS

This 13-hour trip from London to Fort William in Scotland is regarded as a classic railway journey. Historically, overnight trains with sleeping carriages connected cities across the United Kingdom, with a sleeper service having operated on the West Coast Main Line since 1873. As late as the mid-1980s, dozens of sleeper trains travelled along the British network every night. These trains enabled passengers to make the most of the time at their destination as they arrived early in the morning fully refreshed after being gently rocked to sleep on an overnight train. Sadly, most overnight trains have disappeared as a result of changes in passenger travel patterns and the growth of budget airlines. However, thanks to sustained public demand, a few overnight services survive.

This Anglo-Scottish sleeper train was transferred to ScotRail in 1995 after the privatization of British Rail. In 1997, the service was privatized and initially operated by National Express.

The now-nationalized *Caledonian Sleeper* (it was operated by Serco from 2015–2023), is one of Britain's last surviving sleeper services that has been recently upgraded. The new trains evoke a sense of Scotland in both their exterior details and interior design. The Caledonian Double Rooms with a double bed and an en-suite shower are available, as are the more traditional Club and Classic Twin-bunk Rooms. Travellers have the opportunity to sample a taste of Scotland on board with numerous whiskies and culinary dishes served in the Club Car. Guests in Club and Double Rooms also receive Mackie's of Scotland chocolates and Arran Sense of Scotland toiletries.

The *Caledonian Sleeper* operates north of London and serves several Scottish destinations. These services first operated on the Lowland route from London to Edinburgh/Glasgow, and later joined the Highland route to Fort William. The train passes quietly beneath the city of Glasgow on the suburban low-level line in the early hours of the morning before the commuters start using it. Later, once the train has started on the West Highland Line proper, guests can go along to the Club Car and have breakfast while viewing the delights of Loch Long and Cobbler Mountain, shortly followed by Loch Lomond on the other side. After that, it is mountain moor and loch all the way until the train skirts the north side of Ben Nevis and slips into Fort William at 9.57 a.m. in time to catch the morning *Jacobite* steam train to Mallaig. Alternatively, the attractions of Fort William can be visited (page 52).

TRACK NOTES

Typically, a powerful General Motors-built converted Class 73 diesel-electric locomotive, owned and operated by GB Railfreight, hauls the train on beyond Edinburgh and westwards along the estuary of the Clyde River. However, the Glasgow to Inverness service is often hauled by the company's Class 66 locomotives, often used as a double-header, because of the weight of the train and steep gradients. Seated Mark 2 carriages and Mark 3 sleeping cars were replaced, and new carriages were introduced to the rail service.

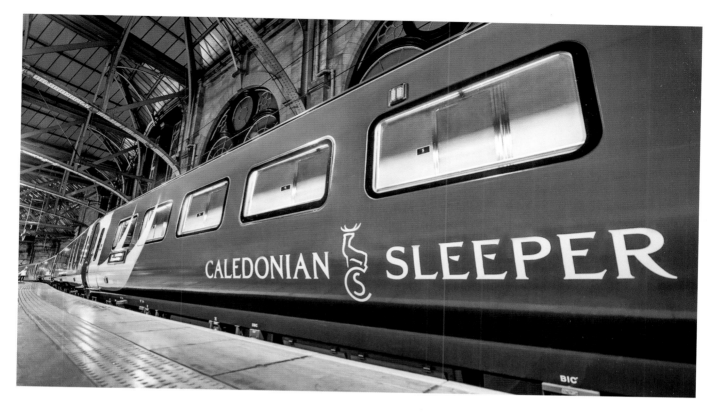

In addition to the *Caledonian Sleeper*, local daytime ScotRail diesel services called Sprinters and the occasional freight train operate along the West Highland Line. ScotRail uses Class 156 Diesel Sprinter Units (DSUs) on this line.

Upgraded sleeping compartments on board the train include handcrafted Glencraft mattresses and en-suite facilities in select accommodation.

WELCOME ABOARD

One of the most exciting rail journeys in Britain is unquestionably the *Caledonian Sleeper* from London to Fort William. The journey begins in Euston Station, possibly London's least inspiring mainline terminal, but the on-train experience makes up for this. This sleeping car train includes well-adorned Mk5 passenger coaches, noted for their excellent ride quality. Unlike the vast majority of train services on the United Kingdom network, which are made up of cramped, self-propelled trains, the sleeping cars on the *Caledonian Sleeper* provide passenger comfort and quality. An onboard host greets guests on the platform and helps them settle into their rooms.

Passengers can arrive at Euston Station well before the departure time, and it is best to arrive early to maximize the experience. The compact sleeping berths are equipped with power points, USB port, sink, tabletop, wardrobe, Glencraft mattress, temperature control, under-the-bed storage space and a bed.

The *Caledonian Sleeper* takes pride in promoting regional food and beverages, and passengers can choose from an extensive selection of Scottish ales, gins and whiskies in the Club Car.

Soon after departure, the train travels into the night along the high-speed West Coast Line. Most passengers are sound asleep as the train passes the historic Crewe Railway crossroads. In the wee hours, the sleepers are shunted at Edinburgh, and from here the line heads inland but continues to follow waterways. The London to Fort William section of the train includes just two sleeping carriages. The Club Car of the London to Aberdeen section of the train is replaced in Edinburgh with another Club Car for the run to Fort William.

At Crianlarich, there is a junction with the line to Oban (page 52). Beyond Crianlarich, the train travels through the wildest and most desolate scenery. It is a stark yet serenely beautiful landscape that constantly changes. On some mornings, the fog and mist cling to the ground, while on others the sky is clear. Author D. H. Lawrence visited the Highlands in 1926 and wrote: 'It is still out of the world, like the very beginning of Europe'.

As the line climbs into the West Highlands, the scenery becomes more impressive. There are few roads on Rannoch Moor, and many of the vistas here can only be seen by train or by taking long hikes. Rannoch Moor Station, located 305 m (1,000 ft) above sea level, is especially remote. Beyond the platforms the line crosses a nine-span, double-intersection, Warren truss bridge on its ascent to Corrour Summit, with Corrour Station situated at 408 m (1,338 ft) above sea level.

Approaching the Bridge of Orchy (Drochaid Urchaidh), the line sweeps through a broad horseshoe curve, and on many mornings the train is bathed in the first rays of sunlight.

The West Highland Line reached Fort William in 1894 but has always been relatively lightly travelled. Historically, train movements were governed by electric train tokens and semaphore signals, but today a modern radio token system ensures train safety as the trains travel along the single-track line. The Bridge of Orchy is one of several places where trains may meet.

The most impressive scenery is on the left-hand side of the train heading north. The *Caledonian Sleeper* may pause here, then begin its descent towards Fort William. The line drops along Loch

Above left Passengers can enjoy the dramatic scenery of the Scottish Highlands along stretches of the line at Dalwhinnie, adjacent to the Cairngorms National Park.

Above right The train passes small villages, such as Bridge of Orchy, where the River Orchy offers one of the finest whitewater rafting sites in the United Kingdom.

Treig, which on clear mornings appears as a crystalline azure mirror. As the line descends, the scenery becomes more wooded, and between Tulloch and Roy Bridge the line transits the confines of a deep, rocky gorge. As the train approaches Fort William, Ben Nevis, the tallest peak in the British Isles at 1,345 m (4,411 ft), looms high on the left.

While Fort William, on the River Lochy, marks the terminus for the *Caledonian Sleeper*, it does not mark the end of the West Highland Line. The train pulls into Fort William at a very respectable 9.57 a.m. to enable passengers to get an early start on the many outdoor adventures and scenic attractions in Fort William. One of the most impressive sights just north of the town is Inverlochy Castle, about which Queen Victoria wrote: 'I never saw a lovelier or more romantic spot.' It is currently closed, but its grandeur can be admired from a distance. In 1901, an extension was built further westwards to the tiny fishing port of Mallaig, perched above a compact, horseshoe-shaped harbour. Local trains work this scenically supreme line three or four times daily.

The Jacobite steam train also operates from Fort William to Mallaig twice daily during its season, from early May until the end of September.

ATTENTION TO DETAIL

The *Caledonian Sleeper* to various Scottish Highland destinations departs at 9.15 p.m. every night of the week except Saturday, as one extended train, which is then split into three sections at Edinburgh for services to Aberdeen, Inverness and Fort William, as well as intermediate destinations along their respective routes.

The *Caledonian Sleeper* provides a sleeper service between London and Fort William. Trains arrive in Fort William at 9.57 a.m. the following day, while train departures from Fort William leave at 7.50 p.m. and arrive at Euston Station at 7.49 a.m. on the following day. The train offers travellers a return to a bygone era and the opportunity to experience a comfortable night's sleep in stylish sleeping rooms. Passengers can arrive two hours before departure and be well settled into their sleeping rooms by the time the train departs.

Various ticket options include seats and sleeping rooms. Sleeping rooms are sold for solo or double accommodation in Double, Club and Classic Rooms. Family tickets are also available. Tickets can be bought online 12 months in advance and are sold as singles (one-way), and travellers seeking a return ticket simply buy two singles.

Up until mid-2023, the train was operated by Serco, a UK-based company that once operated Australia's premier trains, the *Ghan* and the *Indian Pacific*.

Another British sleeper train is the *Night Riviera*, which operates nightly, except on Saturdays, between London's Paddington Station and Penzance in Cornwall.

Below left The rail line now runs to the east of the village of Tomatin, which is the home of Scotland's largest distillery.

Below right The ever-changing scenery along the route includes the Monessie Gorge near the village of Achlauchrach.

BELMOND ROYAL SCOTSMAN

A HIGHLAND FLING

Belmond is an international provider of luxury hotels, cruises and safaris, as well as indulgent rail and river experiences. It operates several luxury trains, including the *Venice Simplon-Orient-Express* (Europe), *British Pullman* (Britain), *Eastern and Oriental Express* (South-east Asia), *Hiram Bingham* (Peru) and *Andean Explorer* (Peru).

The *Royal Scotsman* was launched in 1985 by the Great Scottish and Western Railway Co. (GS&WR), but after five years, the original carriages were retired and replaced by a new set of renovated Pullman cars. In 2007, the train was purchased by Orient-Express Hotels, now known as Belmond, and it is considered one of the world's most luxurious, stylish and innovative trains.

Belmond provides various multi-day train excursions through the Scottish countryside. Its 'Scotland's Classic Splendours' tour is a four-night, all-inclusive, luxurious hotel-on-wheels that travels through picturesque Scotland. The train passes snow-capped peaks and deep valleys, mirrored lochs and stately castles. It immerses guests in a world of myth and legend while they experience timeless luxury on what is regarded as one of the world's most exclusive rail tours.

TRACK NOTES

Up until 2015, the *Royal Scotsman* was hauled mostly by Class 37, Class 47 or Class 57 diesel locomotives operated by West Coast Railways. In 2016, the haulage contract was taken over by GB Railfreight, with two Class 66 locomotives (66743 and 66746) being repainted with *Royal Scotsman, A Belmond Train* detailing.

The train travels throughout the Scottish rail network, and each evening it pulls on to quiet sidings to ensure a restful sleep for passengers. The 10-carriage train carries a maximum of 40 passengers with a guest-to-staff ratio of nearly two to one, making for personalized service. The train, extending more than 206 m (675 ft), comprises an observation/lounge/bar car, two dining cars, a spa car, five accommodation cars and a staff accommodation/generator car.

WELCOME ABOARD

Passengers assemble in Edinburgh on day one to explore its medieval Old Town and elegant Georgian New Town. Belmond provides its guests with a variety of activities, from bike tours, to cooking classes and a gin tour into the Pentland Hills to learn more about the botanicals grown at the Secret Herb Garden and see how they are incorporated into gins produced on a bespoke basis for the *Royal Scotsman*.

On day two, passengers are transferred to Edinburgh Waverley Station's First Class Lounge to drink beverages while completing the journey's formalities. The glistening *Royal Scotsman* awaits, and a kilted Scottish bagpiper sets the mood for a memorable adventure and Highland fling in Scotland's stunning scenery. The train traverses a land of dramatic mountainous peaks, heather-clad hills and mirror-still lochs.

Passengers travel in cabins and carriages that are lined with lacquer-polished wooden marquetry and warm fabrics, which create an Edwardian country-house ambience. En-suite cabins, complete with showers and toilets, provide unparalleled comfort. There are single, twin, double and interconnecting cabins. Double cabins have a large bed, while twin cabins have two single beds. The interconnecting room combines a twin cabin with a double. All cabins are equipped with opening windows, ceiling fan, heating, shower, toilet, toiletries, bathrobe, slippers, towels, woollen tartan blankets, dressing table, wardrobe and hairdryer.

Public cars are as grand, with Scottish-motif mahogany marquetry, carpeted floors and plush drapes. The lounge Observation Car is the epicentre of social activity on the journey. It is fitted out with comfortable sofas and armchairs in which guests can drink complimentary beverages (alcoholic and non-alcoholic). This car also includes an open-air observation platform at the rear of the Observation Car, which is a delight for photographers. Whisky drinkers can partake of a wee dram from the numerous

offerings, including many from Scotland's west coast, such as Oban, Lagavulin and Talisker. Musicians and guest speakers also entertain guests in the evening.

Passengers dine on memorable meals prepared by chefs with Michelin-star experience. Locally sourced produce such as classic kedgeree, seafood, pigeon, Highland lamb and beef feature. Meals are complemented by specially selected wines and premium liqueurs. The Bamford Haybarn Spa car is set up for further indulgence, should any be needed.

Once the piper's pipes fall silent, the train departs Edinburgh crossing the Forth Bridge over the Firth of Forth. This UNESCO World Heritage Site to the west of Edinburgh is regarded as Scotland's greatest built structure. The cantilever bridge is an

The *Royal Scotsman* passes through the picturesque Scottish Highlands and across famous viaducts that have featured in several blockbuster movies.

iconic sight, and the train moves slowly across it, enabling passengers to admire its grandeur.

On its way to Keith, the train passes Dundee, Arbroath, Montrose and Aberdeen. It crosses the Tay Bridge on its approach to Dundee, and observant passengers may notice the remnants of the first bridge, which collapsed in 1897, taking the lives of 72 passengers on a train that was crossing during a storm. With a population of some 200,000, Aberdeen is a major port that services the North Sea oil and gas industry. The train arrives in the town of Keith in time for dinner and a peaceful overnight rest after a nightcap of Speyside whisky produced at one of the town's four distilleries. Rail enthusiasts may want to return here to ride on the Keith and Dufftown Railway – the Whisky Line; a Scottish heritage railway (opposite).

On the third day, the train heads towards Inverness on the scenic Kyle of Lochalsh Line. The train journeys to Strathcarron and passengers can choose to alight here to visit the picturesque Attadale Gardens, or to remain on the train to alight later at the fishing village of Plockton on Loch Carron to view a seal colony. The gardens, lined with ponds, paths, craggy cliffs and sculptures, provide vistas over the sea to the Isle of Skye. Everyone gathers that evening for a formal train dinner in the sleepy fishing village of Kyle of Lochalsh.

After breakfast the next day, passengers are driven by coach to the impressive thirteenth-century Eilean Castle, perched on an island where three lochs meet. The restored castle has featured in films including the 1999 James Bond film, *The World is Not Enough*. Rejoining the train, Garve is the next stop to sample the liquid delights at Glen Ord Distillery. It has operated under various names, and its whisky is now branded Singleton of Glen Ord. The next stop is Carrbridge on the Highland Main Line for the sixteenth-century Ballindalloch Castle. Passengers rejoin the train at Boat of Garten, where dinner is served overlooking the River Spey. The heritage Strathspey Railway operates along a section of the track between Aviemore and Broomhill.

After breakfast on day five, a visit is made to the thirteenth-century Rothiemurchas Estate for fishing, clay-pigeon shooting and an estate tour. Afterwards, lunch is served on the train as it travels between Kingussie and Dunkeld. During lunch, the train crosses the Druimuachdar Pass at 452 m (1,484 ft), the highest point on the British rail network. After the pass, there is an off-train visit to Glamis Castle. The castle was the inspiration for Shakespeare's *Macbeth* and was the Scottish childhood home of HM Queen Elizabeth, the Queen Mother, the birthplace of HRH Princess Margaret and a royal holiday retreat. After a castle tour, passengers are driven to Perth by coach for a formal dinner on the train. On the morning of the sixth day, they travel back to Edinburgh by train and disembark.

ATTENTION TO DETAIL

Journeys on the *Royal Scotsman* are inclusive of meals, beverages, accommodation, guides, entrance fees, and off-train activities and excursions. Premium tariffs reflect the train's exclusivity and dressing accordingly for the occasion is recommended, especially a jacket for men. The train can be chartered for exclusive journeys for groups of 40, while scheduled journeys depart from April to October.

Belmond makes dreams come true with its legendary hotels and a once-in-a-lifetime train journey. The United Kingdom's only luxury multi-day sleeper train combines Edwardian elegance with the comforts of a country house.

Opposite top Belmond's *Royal Scotsman*, the United Kingdom's only luxury multi-day sleeper train, travels past expansive lochs and the magnificent countryside of the Scottish Highlands.

Opposite bottom The open-air veranda in the observation car enables passengers on the *Royal Scotsman* to get closer to the Scottish countryside.

KEITH & DUFFTOWN RAILWAY

Britain's most northerly heritage railway proceeds for 17.7 km (11 miles) from Dufftown to historic Keith. Dufftown is regarded as the world's malt whisky capital, and this railway relives the true spirit of Scotland

Dufftown was founded in 1817 by the Earl of Fife, with its high-quality water being an essential ingredient for the development of local distilling. Today, Dufftown's most famous export is Glenfiddich, which is the only Highland single malt whisky to be distilled, matured and bottled on one site. The distillery, beside the track in Dufftown, has, for five generations, been run by the Grant family and is open to the public in the summer, where the whisky-making process can be viewed. The ramparts of the thirteenth-century Balvenie Castle are close by.

On leaving Dufftown, the line passes to the rear of the distillery and under the walls of Balvenie Castle, before heading across the Fiddich Viaduct over the River Fiddich. The train makes the steep ascent to the 180 m (590 ft) summit that marks the watershed between the tributaries of the Fiddich and the source of the River Isla. Heading down from the summit, the valley opens on to Loch Park. The route passes through rolling hills, pine forests, deep glens and fields of barley.

The 'Dram Tram' is housed in a coach that has been converted for functions, parties and whisky tastings. The interior stays true to the railway's history as the Whisky Line, with tartan curtains and carpets, plus furniture made from recycled whisky casks sourced from Speyside Cooperage.

The line is staffed by volunteers and operates on most Fridays, Saturdays and Sundays from Easter through the beginning of October. There are three daily trains, with the first departure from Dufftown at 10.30 a.m. and the last return from Keith at 4.30 p.m. The journey takes 40 minutes. Standard and first-class seating is available, as well as cream teas and sparkling wine. Charter journeys are available, as are themed trains like Santa Specials, Ghost Trains and the Whisky Festival.

NORTH YORKSHIRE MOORS RAILWAY

BRITAIN'S MOST POPULAR HERITAGE RAILWAY

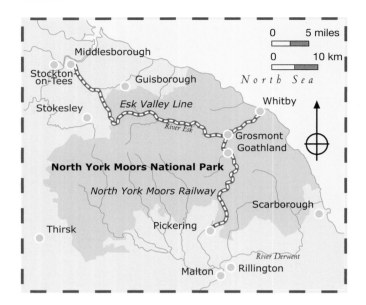

The North Yorkshire Moors Railway (NYMR) is a heritage railway that passes through the North York Moors National Park. It first opened in 1836 as the Whitby and Pickering Railway. This line was conceived by George Stephenson in 1831 in order to open up inland trade routes from Whitby, which was a significant port at that time.

The line between Grosmont and Rillington was closed in 1965, but the line between Grosmont and Pickering was reopened in 1973 by the North York Moors Historical Railway Trust Ltd. In 2007, the railway started operating regular services over a 9.7 km (6 mile) section of the Esk Valley Line north of Grosmont to Whitby. The railway is owned and operated by a charitable trust with 100 full-time employees, supported by seasonal staff and hundreds of volunteers. It is a not-for-profit charity run as part of the local community. Daily operations are carried out by volunteers who have railway operations and business experience. The railway carries 300,000 passengers annually, making it Britain's most popular heritage railway. Every passenger helps preserve one of the world's earliest and most historic railways.

TRACK NOTES

The railway extends from Pickering to coastal Whitby over a distance of 38.6 km (24 miles). One-way journeys take 100 minutes.

Steam and heritage diesel train journeys enable passengers to take in Yorkshire's amazing scenery and sights.

The iconic locomotive No. 4498 'Sir Nigel Gresley' has rejoined the railway after a seven-year overhaul. Passengers can also ride in authentic teak carriages. Other steam locomotives include BR Standard 4 Tank, 9F, Repton and BR Standard 4 MT, and passengers seeking specific locomotives should consult the railway's website for the schedule; however, the NYMR reserves the right to make changes.

WELCOME ABOARD

The journey can be made from Pickering to Whitby, in reverse, or from Pickering to Whitby and back. The Whitby Abbey ruins overlook the bustling harbour at the River Esk's mouth. The town is known for its quirky, narrow streets and the Captain Cook Memorial Museum. Visitors can learn about the seafarer who once lived here and charted the coasts of New Zealand and eastern Australia.

From Whitby, the train travels through windswept dales and across rolling moors. It stops at Grosmont Station, which is home to the railway's operating and engineering sections. Steam and diesel locomotives are serviced and restored in the shed, which is accessible through the George Stephenson Tunnel, built in 1835.

Grosmont Station is located at the junction where the heritage railway ends and the main network begins. The Esk Valley Line connects both Middlesbrough and Whitby to the NYMR.

The next stop is Goathland Station, made famous as Hogsmeade Station in the 2001 film *Harry Potter and the Sorcerer's Stone*. It was also known as Aidensfield in the television programme *Heartbeat*. Goathland village, with its shops and pubs, is just a few minutes' walk away. From here, visitors can explore the national park by walking along the rail trail back to Grosmont or to the Mallyan Spout Waterfall. Goathland Station has a shop and tea room located in a converted 1922-style shed.

Trains only stop at Newtondale Halt on request. The 1912-styled heritage Levisham Station, surrounded by the national park, is the next stop. Its Weighbridge Tea Hut is only open on weekends and public holidays, and for special events.

Pickering Station is a heritage railway station dating back to the steam era of the 1930s. A highlight is the impressive roof structure, which has been reinstated to the design of the 1847 original. The station has a souvenir shop and tea room serving snacks, drinks and ice-creams. Pickering stages a market every Monday while Beck Isle Museum, close to the station, features the history and culture of the town. Its marketplace is lined with small shops, and the thirteenth-century castle is worth visiting.

Above Goathland Station features in various *Harry Potter* movies as the *Hogwarts Express* Station at Hogsmeade.

Opposite The railway passes through the North York National Park with one of the nation's largest expanses of heather woodland.

NYMR offers accommodation in two cosy camping coaches situated at Levisham and Goathland Stations, along with Station House at Grosmont.

ATTENTION TO DETAIL

Daily trains operate between Whitby and Pickering, and fares vary throughout the season. The best prices are provided via the railway's website, and advanced bookings are recommended. Discounted rates for pre-booked groups of 20 or more in reserved seating are available.

The train hosts numerous special days, activities and events. During the train's experience days, it is possible to ride on a steam locomotive footplate. An annual steam gala is staged over four days in September, while in October a light spectacular illuminates the train at Pickering Station.

Special Santa trains are featured throughout December. Pullman Dining Car Service provides fine dining as the train proceeds on its journey.

SETTLE–CARLISLE RAILWAY

ENGLAND'S MOST SCENIC RAILWAY

In his insightful and humorous book *The Road to Little Dribbling*, author Bill Bryson notes that the Settle–Carlisle line (S&C) may be both the most picturesque and the most wonderfully unnecessary railway line ever built in England. The scenery is characterized by rolling hills with sparse vegetation, a mix of bogs, grasses and moss, but very few trees or built structures. Over a third of the route weaves through the scenic Yorkshire Dales National Park of austere rolling hills and lush, verdant valleys, while stone-built farm buildings and herds of cows are found around the edges of the moorland.

Britain's highly acclaimed Settle and Carlisle line made the news when the old nationalized British Rail tried to discontinue the route. It attempted this twice, first in the 1960s and again in the 1980s. The popularity of the line secured first its survival, then its revival in recent years. Several stations along the line that had been closed during the lean years (for example, Dent Station was closed for 16 years) have been restored and reopened, while the line's infrastructure has also been renewed and improved.

Work began on the S&C railway in 1869 but was not completed until 1876. The railway is the product of the Midland Railway's expansion towards the Scottish border. The line was among the last significant main lines constructed in England, and building it was an arduous task because of the remote terrain. The often harsh weather did not help, and fences beside the track in exposed mountain areas prevent snow from drifting across the track. For practical reasons, the line did not always go close to the settlements it was designed to serve. For example, Dent and Kirkby Stations are some distance from their respective towns.

The line opened in 1876, more than half a century after George Stephenson's Stockton and Darlington had spurred the nation into a frenzied state in which almost every sizable village in Britain was linked by rail. The route was built primarily to serve express trains and did so at the expense of communities along the line. S&C's engineers followed the most efficient profile to minimize gradients, rather than build the line to connect town centres. However, this often placed local stations at an inconvenient distance from the towns along the route. The lack of nearby villages on the central portion of the line accentuates its desolate, windswept qualities.

TRACK NOTES

Rugged terrain demanded a highly engineered line, and the S&C route of 116 km (72 miles) features 14 tunnels, 325 small bridges and 21 viaducts (defined as a long, multi-span bridge). Well before privatization, British Rail operated long, locomotive-hauled trains such as the Class 47 along this route. The use of steam locomotives on the line ended in 1968, but since then the S&C has been a favourite for historical excursions. Many of Britain's most famous locomotives, like the *Flying Scotsman*, have hauled trains on the line, and some still operate to give visitors a classic rail experience. Northern Rail assigns Class 158 diesel rail cars on its Leeds–Settle–Carlisle services.

Most of the stations and infrastructure on the line date from its original construction, while the use of traditional upper quadrant semaphore signals to manage train movements adds to the line's nostalgic appeal. The railway infrastructure is owned by Network Rail and operated by Northern Rail Limited. Some stations are

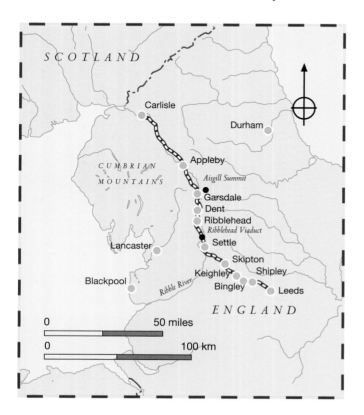

privately owned, while others are leased to the Settle and Carlisle Railway Trust.

The train passes through Dentdale, a dale (valley) in the north-west of the Yorkshire Dales National Park in Cumbria.

WELCOME ABOARD

The railway line to Carlisle starts in the Yorkshire market town of Settle, 380 km (236 miles) north of London. The entire line is noted for its scenic splendour and is dotted with noteworthy railway infrastructure. Arguably the most interesting section of the route is between Settle and Garsdale, where the railway passes through the Yorkshire Dales National Park. Settle Station opened in 1876 and was just one of three stations serving the line's namesake town. Settle, Appleby and Carlisle are the only staffed stations along the route. There is a souvenir shop at the historic station, and its water tower has been converted into a private residence.

The line runs northwards, following the Ribble Valley through Stainforth and Helwith Bridge. Horton-in-Ribblesdale is one of several stations that were closed in the 1960s and '70s, but it was reopened in 1986. Beyond Horton, the line assumes its iconic

image, crossing windswept pastures and bogs against the backdrop of the Three Peaks of the Yorkshire Dales.

Ribblehead Station is where passengers can alight to get close to the line's most impressive structure, the famed 24-arch Ribblehead Viaduct (or Batty Moss) across the Ribble River. Measuring 402 m (1,319 ft) in length and 50.6 m (106 ft) tall, this is the longest bridge along the route and was built using one and a half million bricks and numerous limestone blocks. British Rail wanted to replace it with a modern steel bridge, but sanity prevailed, the stone and brick edifice was restored, and the iconic scene remains unblemished. Its backdrop of Pen-y-ghent Mountain, one of the Three Yorkshire Peaks, makes the setting even more spectacular. Despite Ribblehead's remote location in the middle of the Yorkshire Dales National Park, there are a few other attractions in addition to the railway station with its cafe and visitors centre. The Ribblehead Station Inn, within walking distance, offers refreshing ales, excellent pub fare (try the steak 'n' ale pie) and accommodation. The famous

Ribblehead Viaduct is a short walk away, as are the remains of the old shanty camp where some 3,000 navvies were housed during the construction of the railway.

At Blea Moor, the line crosses a watershed divide in Blea Moor Tunnel, the longest on the line, measuring 2,404 m (7,887 ft). Looming above the tunnel is Ingleborough, which rises to 723 m (2,372 ft) and is the second highest of the Three Yorkshire Peaks. Immediately north of the tunnel is the impressive Dent Head Viaduct (182 m / 597 ft long and 30.5 m / 100 ft high) with 10 arches. Dent Station sits at 350 m (1,150 ft) above sea level, making it one of the highest mainline stations in the United Kingdom (at 452 m / 1,484 ft, Scotland's Druimuachdar Pass is the highest point on the British rail network, page 37). The old station buildings here have been converted into holiday accommodation. Beyond Dent, the line crests at Ais Gill (Summit) at 356 m (1,169 ft), then drops steadily as it continues to the north. The most impressively situated station is at Garsdale, which, while slightly lower than Dent, seems to rest on top of the world. S&C's tallest bridge is the magnificent 12-arch limestone Smardale Viaduct, which rises 40 m (131 ft) above Scandal Beck.

The train passes through the Cumbrian Fells and the pastoral Eden Valley. It is possible to alight at one of several intermediate stations to explore the surroundings, or to return to Settle on one of Britain's most beloved lines. While scheduled passenger services are relatively infrequent compared with more populated lines in the UK, there are ample trains to allow exploration at various locations. In addition to passenger traffic, the line is a favoured freight corridor for coal and aggregate trains.

The train pulls into Carlisle Station, where passengers can explore the ancient Cumbrian town close to the Scottish border. Some sections of the town date back to the Roman era. Its relatively intact castle and prison once hosted Mary, Queen of Scots. Known as the 'Great Border Town', it has been a military stronghold for centuries. Carlisle became an important mill town in the nineteenth century, with its railway being a strategic link to the outside world. Once, the lines of seven railway companies converged on Carlisle Citadel Railway Station, and its marshalling yards were, for a time, Europe's largest. The adjoining Carlisle Railway Station is regarded as one of England's most important early railway stations.

ATTENTION TO DETAIL

Connections from the British Rail network in Leeds and Lancaster make the S&C Line easy to reach. Trains operate every two to three hours, and the journey takes about 105 minutes.

Even when it is raining, this train ride still promises incredible scenery, as the rain adds interest, especially when the surrounding waterfalls are in full flow.

A special 'Settle and Carlisle Day Ranger' ticket is available to enable unlimited travel between stations at Skipton and Carlisle. This means that passengers can hop on and off trains at their leisure and experience the many highlights of the line by train and on foot. For example, there is a half-day walk between Dent and Ribblehead Stations.

A private operator, Rail Charter Services, provides occasional luxury coach travel between Skipton and Carlisle. Facilities include a restaurant car, reclining leather seating, panoramic windows and disabled access on its *Staycation Express* trains.

Today, the S&C carries more passengers than it did historically, and for many good reasons. It is popular with railway enthusiasts, hikers and tourists, and carries well over one million passengers annually. It is one of Britain's finest preserved rail lines and offers a trip back to a bygone era.

Opposite Settle Railway Station was built in 1876 and is very close to the centre of the small market town of Settle.

Left Rail Charter Services operates charter journeys on the route using a dedicated 2+5 HST set, with all first-class carriages and a dining car.

SNOWDON MOUNTAIN RAILWAY

THE UNITED KINGDOM'S ONLY RACK AND PINION RAILWAY

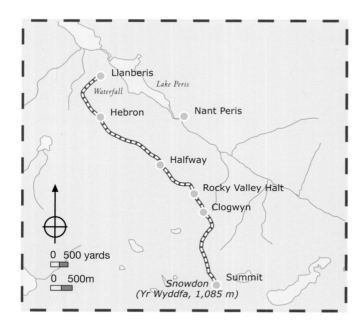

The Snowdon Mountain Railway uses rack-and-pinion (cogwheel) traction similar to this to help it ascend the steep sections of the line.

The Snowdon Mountain Railway (SMR) is one of several fascinating Welsh narrow-gauge railways. The railway, located in Llanberis, transports passengers up to Mount Snowdon (Yr Wyddfa) in northern Snowdonia. The highest peak in Wales and England is also the most popular mountain in the United Kingdom, with more than 600,000 annual visitors. Perhaps not surprisingly, the view from the 1,085 m (3,560 ft) summit is also regarded as its most spectacular. Mount Snowdon also forms part of a walk called the National Three Peaks Challenge.

Visitors have been travelling to Llanberis since 1896 to experience the unique rail journey that ascends Mount Snowdon. This is also the only public rack-and-pinion railway in the British Isles and is often regarded as one of the world's most unique and wonderful railway journeys.

TRACK NOTES

The railway services include both a heritage steam-locomotive experience and traditional diesel services. The railway's rack-and-pinion system is of key interest to train enthusiasts, especially as the SMR is the only public rack-and-pinion railway in the British Isles.

Traction on steep slopes is challenging and often unsuitable for a normal adhesion railway. A solution to this potential problem was to use a toothed rack between the running rails to provide a cog (pinion) on the locomotive to enable it to traverse steep gradients.

While there are several different types of railway rack-and-pinion system, the one preferred at Snowdon and in many other global locations is the Abt System, invented in 1885 by Dr Roman Abt, a Swiss railway engineer. This system uses less steel than others and is therefore less expensive to manufacture and install.

The Snowdon Rack System utilizes a pair of toothed racks offset by one tooth and two driven axles on each locomotive, each axle with a pair of pinions. Safety is thus ensured, because two teeth are always fully engaged. The brakes also use the rack to slow and stop the train, with the brakes fitted to the pinion axles on the locomotive and the carriages.

Because the Snowdon track was designed in Switzerland in 1895, metric measurements were adopted. The track gauge is 800 mm (2 ft 7½ in), which is common for most mountain railways. The route traverses a mostly single track with three passing loops.

The railway is 7.5 km (4.5 miles) long and has an average

gradient of 1 in 7.86 (the steepest gradient is 1 in 5.5). The train moves at an average speed of 8 km/h (5 mph).

The railway currently operates four coal-fired steam locomotives manufactured by the Swiss Locomotive and Machine Works of Winterhur, north-east of Zurich. Three are original locomotives dating from 1895 and 1896, while the remaining one was built in 1922.

Four British-built diesel locomotives were acquired between 1986 and 1992 to complement the fleet of steam locomotives. Six-cylinder turbocharged Rolls Royce diesel engines power these locomotives, manufactured by Hunslet Engine Company of Leeds.

WELCOME ABOARD

The original carriages were open above waist level and had canvas curtains, which provided little protection from the mountain's variable weather. These were later modified to create enclosed bodies. Each carriage had a capacity of 56 passengers and a guard. The driver provides commentary on the way up to the mountain.

'Wyddfa' locomotive was built at the Swiss Locomotive and Machine Works in Winterhur, Switzerland.

Between 2012 and 2013, seven new carriages, each accommodating 74 passengers, were delivered, followed by three more in 2013. These were designed and built in a partnership between Garmendale Engineering Limited of Ilkeston, Derbyshire, and the Hunslet Engine Company. Four carriages also provide wheelchair access.

ATTENTION TO DETAIL

Trains depart Llanberis Station and haul passengers at a steady pace to the summit. Here, a 30-minute stopover allows passengers time to take in the panoramic view. There are five additional stations between Llanberis and the summit. Early-bird discounts are available on the first diesel departure at 9 a.m. From then, diesel trains depart every 30 minutes, and there are just three steam

FACINATING NARROW-GAUGE WELSH RAILWAYS

Wales has several other fascinating narrow-gauge railways that are now popular with tourists. The Ffestiniog Railway, the world's oldest surviving narrow-gauge railway (operated by the oldest surviving train company), was built in 1832 to service the local slate industry. The steam-locomotive journey of 75 minutes commences in harbourside Porthmadog and travels 22.7 km (13.5 miles) to the quarrying town of Blaenau Ffestiniog. During its 213 m (700 ft) scenic ascent, partly through Snowdonia National Park, it passes farms, rivers, forests, waterfalls and lakes. A looping spiral section is especially exciting. The railway is an integral part of the UNESCO Slate Landscape of North Wales World Heritage Site.

Ffestiniog Railway's sister service, the Welsh Highlands Railway, travels 40 km (25 miles) between Porthmadog and Caernarfon, making it the longest heritage railway in the United Kingdom. Passengers can sit in a luxurious First Class Pullman carriage and enjoy a meal on their journey. Trains to the foot of Snowdon pass the village of Beddgelert and travel over the Aberglaslyn Pass.

The Talyllyn Railway, established to ship slate from a quarry to market, is now a tourist train. The pace of rural life in the countryside through which the train passes is as slow as the train. This train operates from Tywyn to Abergynolwyn and Nant Gwernol. It passes through Fathew Valley and past Dolgoch Falls. Original locomotives and open-sided carriages add to the thrill of the journey.

Llanberis Lake Railway, in the heart of Snowdonia, is a short journey of 8 km (5 miles) to Penllyn, passing the thirteenth-century Dolbadarn Castle and Lake Padarn, and providing views of Mount Snowdon. Passengers can alight at Gilfach Ddu to admire the National Slate Museum or Cei Llydan by the lake.

locomotive departures per day, with the first leaving at 10.30 a.m.

Most passengers are tourists travelling on pre-booked tickets, with weekends and the main summer holiday months being especially busy.

Station Buffet and Platform Grill at Llanberis Station is licensed and sells beverages and snacks. A gift shop is located in the original booking hall, which dates back to 1896.

A cafe and visitors' centre were opened at the summit in 2009 to provide shelter, snacks and beverages. There is also a cafe at Halfway Station. The railway is operated by Heritage Great Britain, and bookings are recommended, especially for peak times. Ticket prices for heritage steam-train journeys are higher than for diesel locomotive journeys. For logistical purposes, passengers must return on the same train that they travelled on to the summit, or walk back to the base station. Repositioning steam trains at Llanberis Station takes longer than for diesel-driven locomotives, so that the former operate every three hours. Diesel train services are also more economical to operate.

The railway closes from November to mid-March, and services can be curtailed during the season due to inclement weather. Weather is a major factor in enjoying all that Snowdon has to offer. The weather can be windy, chilly and variable at the summit, and passengers need to be prepared for such eventualities. It can be misty with limited visibility, and during the summer it may be quite hot and the carriages can be stuffy. The vagaries of the weather are beyond the control of the train's operators, but all passengers agree that on a fine day the views are spectacular.

Promotional journeys and activities are also on offer. In September 2018, Switzerland Tourism brought a steam locomotive from Switzerland to SMR for a month-long celebration to mark 126 years since the trains were last together.

It was discovered that the locomotive currently operating on Switzerland's Brienz Rothorn Bahn was built in the same factory as the locomotives operating on Snowdon. The Brienz Rothorn Bahn is a rack railway that departs from Brienz, at the eastern end of Lake Brienz, to the summit of the Brienzer Rothorn. It has been operational since 1892 and is Switzerland's only daily steam rack railway.

Opposite top The new building for the Summit Station was erected in 2009 and named Hafod Eryri.

Opposite bottom A train on the Snowdon Mountain Railway inching its way along a ridge to the mountain summit.

SEVERN VALLEY RAILWAY

RESCUED FROM TOTAL OBLIVION

The Severn, Britain's longest river, flows for 354 km (220 miles) through Wales and England before entering the Celtic Sea via the Bristol Channel. The region played an important role in the Industrial Revolution of the eighteenth century. For example, Coalbrookdale on the Severn was the location of an early, intensive iron industry and is also the site of the famous cast-iron Iron Bridge erected by John Wilkinson and Abraham Darby and opened in 1781. This was the world's first cast-iron bridge and inspired many others around the world.

The evolution of the iron and coal industries was key to the development of British steam railways in the early nineteenth century. The Severn Valley Railway (SVR), situated downriver from Coalbrookdale, is one of Britain's most loved lines. It extends for 16.5 miles (26.5 km) through a scenic section of its namesake valley.

The line took nine years to build and opened in 1862. Originally, it was part of the much longer Shrewsbury to Hartlebury Line. The original single-track line had 15 stations and did not have the Bewdley to Kidderminster section until the loop line was constructed and opened in June 1878 by the Great Western Railway (GWR), which operated much of the rail network in south and mid-Wales. For more than a century, this line operated with limited capacity and was a lightly used through route connecting Shrewsbury with Bewdley and Kidderminster. It mostly served mines, with coal transported from several coalfields in the area to nearby power stations and further afield.

Its scenery was also appreciated by train travellers, but passenger numbers began dwindling in the 1920s. British Railways (BR) took over the railway after a government-nationalized programme in 1948. Diesel units replaced steam locomotives, but by the 1960s the line was a shadow of its glory days. Continued British government rationalization led to the closure of many lines. This short-sighted severing of passenger services on the SVR as a through-route occurred in 1963.

A local plan was hatched two years later by the Severn Valley Railway Society (SVRS) to save the line from oblivion. In 1966,

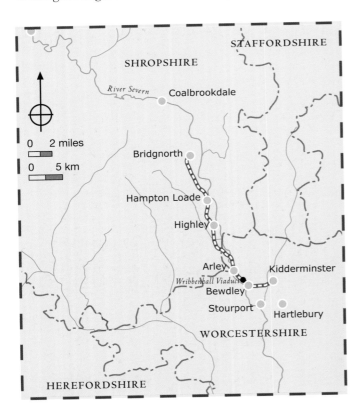

the SVRS purchased the line from BR, and a year later the first locomotive was sourced. No. 3205 was the first of four that entered the inventory, including The Flying Pig (43106), which still operates on the line. In 1970, the first train of the preserved railway operated between Bridgnorth and Hampton Loade. Other parts of the closed line were acquired by the SVR, including Bewdley (1974) and finally Kidderminster (1984). The former BR goods yard at Comberton Hill was repurposed as the new Kidderminster Town Station. In 1984, the line was restored from Bridgnorth to Kidderminster, where it connects with the mainline network.

TRACK NOTES

The mostly volunteer-operated railway has developed into one of Britain's finest historical lines. In addition to tracks and trains, SVR includes faithfully restored passenger stations and signal boxes, engine sheds and other period-railway infrastructure, allowing enthusiasts the opportunity to travel back to an era when Britain's railways reigned supreme. The SVR runs trains using

Above 4930 Hagley Hall (named after Hagley Hall in Worcestershire) is a Great Western Railway, 4-6-0 Hall Class locomotive, built in 1929 at Swindon Works, Wiltshire.

Opposite The Severn Valley Railway Society was formed in 1965 by members seeking to preserve a section of the line which had closed in 1963 and volunteers still make an invaluable contribution.

numerous serviceable steam locomotives and more than five dozen restored carriages that span various periods.

The railway collection includes several operative and non-operative steam and diesel locomotives, including steam locos such as the SR34027 Taw Valley, GWR2857 Heavy Goods Loco and LMS Ivatt Class 43106. Most of the SVR staff who play a vital role in operating the railway are volunteers.

WELCOME ABOARD

A charitable trust operates the Kidderminster Railway Museum located in the former GWR warehouse just beyond platform two at Kidderminster Town Station. Arrive early for the SVR journey

and take time to inspect an extensive collection of railway memorabilia, which dates back to the steam age. Nearby in the station ground, the Coalyard Miniature Railway is something for the whole family to enjoy. This 184 mm (7¼ in) gauge aluminium track on plastic sleepers is 357 m (1,171 ft) long, and runs alongside the SVR platforms. The railway also operates a range of battery, steam and petrol-driven locomotives.

Trains begin their journey northwards to Bridgnorth by skirting south of Kidderminster before passing through the Bewdley Tunnel, and passing the West Midland Safari Park on the right-hand side on their way to Bewdley, which is itself an old junction station and features two working signal boxes, one at each end of the station. The town is a well-preserved Georgian town, mostly on the western side of the River Severn, while the station is on the eastern bank. Alight here for the Bewdley Museum, Victoria Gardens and perhaps the possibility of seeing former Led Zeppelin lead singer Robert Plant playing tennis at the club, of which he is a member.

The magnificent eight-arch Wribbenhall Viaduct is located just north of Bewdley Station. The line winds for another 6.5 km (4 miles) towards Arley, crossing the cast-iron Victoria Bridge over the River Severn just before reaching the station. Arley retains all the charm of a classic rural railway station and makes for a perfect mid-trip stop for those who want to alight to break their journey. Like many of SVR's stations, this one features a passing loop and active signal box. Several pleasant walks are possible from Arley, including the 4 km (2.5 mile) Upper Arley Circular Walk that takes in the arboretum. Cross the footbridge over the rail line and follow the ferryman logo for the circuit walk. Alternatively, walk down the road near the station and stop at the Harbour Inn for a refreshing ale, afternoon tea, or steak and ale pie in the beer garden overlooking the river. For those who can wait, the Railwayman's Arms is located at Bridgnorth Station at the line's terminus.

Beyond Arley, the line continues upriver for 4 km (2.5 miles) to Highley, which is the location of another passing loop, a small yard and the SVR Engine House Visitor Centre. Admission is free, and it is open from 10.30 a.m. to 5 p.m. on operating days. The yard houses famous locomotives, and delicious food is served in the refreshment rooms. An on-train buffet also operates, and special dining experiences like the three-course Sunday lunch are offered throughout the year.

Above A steam train crossing the Victoria Bridge over the Severn River in Worcestershire.

Opposite A diesel-hauled train passing through the small hamlet of Hampton Loade in Shropshire.

After another 3.2 km (2 miles), the line reaches the quiet station for the hamlet of Hampton Loade in Shropshire. A further 6.4 km (4 miles) along the train reaches the end of the line at Bridgnorth. The pleasant combination of rural scenery, slow-paced vintage trains and classic villages makes for one of the world's most memorable railway experiences. While a round trip can be accomplished in as little as three hours, many visitors choose to spend the whole day exploring various opportunities on the train, at the Engine House or in villages along the route.

ATTENTION TO DETAIL

The best way to access the SVR is to arrive at Kidderminster via a mainline service. SVR operates a seasonal schedule varying from four to seven round trips each day. Extra trains are made available for special events and charters. In the winter, the services are limited, with trains only operating on certain days. It is best to choose a day with a full complement of trains to allow for stopovers at stations along the line.

Pre-booked Freedom of the Line tickets for adults, children and families are the best options for those who want to alight and explore the towns along the route as well as the Engine House

Visitor Centre at Highley. Single point-to-point tickets are also available. Wheelchair access is provided, even in the original heritage carriages.

Themed journeys are possible, with Murder Mysteries, Footplate Experience (the opportunity to drive a locomotive), Ghost Train (Halloween), Christmas and various dining options available. Christmas is a special time with various services in operation, including Steam in Lights, Santa Trains, Carol Trains and festive dining departures.

The SVR offers more than preserved steam and heritage diesel locomotives – it provides the experience of a classic British branch from the pre-grouping GWR network in the 1930s and '40s. Visitors can admire beautifully preserved stations, lovingly restored carriages, and historic local towns as they travel through Worcestershire and Shropshire. This small backwater line has been transformed into one of the nation's leading heritage railways, attracting tourists and rail enthusiasts from around the world.

WEST HIGHLAND LINE

GLASGOW TO MALLAIG

The West Highland Line from Glasgow to Mallaig in Scotland travels more than 264 km (164 miles) and takes almost five and a half hours. While travelling this route, it is also worth considering taking the line from Crianlarich to Oban and back. Many parts of the journey are only possible via train, so this is the best way to see a mostly unseen part of Scotland. The route heads north towards the West Coast and through Loch Lomond and the Trossachs National Park. The line splits at Crianlarich, proceeding past Loch Awe to Oban or high up to Rannoch Moor, through remote wilderness and on to Mallaig. Many consider this journey through Scotland to be the most scenic of all railways in the United Kingdom.

The *Royal Scotsman* and *The Jacobite* steam trains also operate on sections of this line (page 34).

TRACK NOTES

ScotRail Class 153 and Class 156 diesel multiple units (DMUs) operate along this line. A unique feature of these coaches is that bicycles, sporting gear and heavy luggage can be accommodated. Trains travel between Glasgow's Queen Street and Mallaig. In summer, the popular *The Jacobite* steam-hauled trains, operated by West Coast Railways, journey along the line between Fort William and Mallaig.

WELCOME ABOARD

The West Highland Line traverses some of Scotland's wildest scenery, which ranges from near-deserted moors to forested lochs and crumbling castles. When the line leaves the Glasgow suburban network at Craigendoran it climbs high above Loch Long, with wonderful views of the Cobbler Mountain, Loch Lomond and Tyndrum, where Scotland's only gold mine is located. Other highlights are Horseshoe Curve and Viaduct below Ben Dorain, Rannoch Moor, Corrour (Britain's highest mainline station), Loch Treig and then through Monessie Gorge and waterfall before a final descent around the north side of Ben Nevis into Fort William.

At Crianlarich, a decision needs to be made to continue to Oban or to travel directly to Mallaig via Fort William. The decision for single malt-whisky lovers is easy, as Oban is home to one of Scotland's smallest and oldest distilleries, dating back to 1794. On

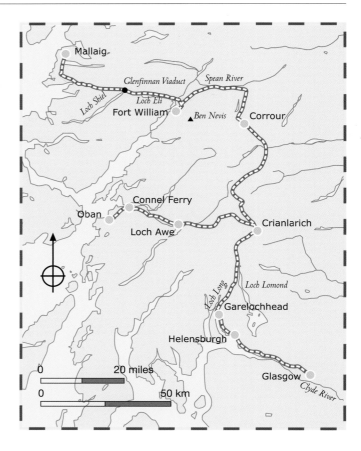

its journey to Oban, the train passes the north edge of Loch Awe, in the shadow of Ben Cruachan. The ruins of the fifteenth-century Kilchurn Castle are visible at the head of Loch Awe. The train proceeds from the loch along the River Awe towards Loch Etive. At Connel, the train passes the rapids of the Falls of Lora and the impressive Connel Bridge.

In Oban, passengers can visit the Oban Distillery for an intimate whisky experience within sight of the little bay, which 'Oban' means in Gaelic. Whisky from the Oban Distillery is considered one of the six classic West Highland whiskies. Distillers will happily suggest a whisky pairing for the district's famous seafood. Other attractions in town include the popular beach of Ganavan Sands, McCaig's Tower, the waterfront along Corran Esplanade, Dunollie Castle and Castle Stalker, which was featured in the film *Monty Python and the Holy Grail*. Ferries depart Oban for Mull, Iona and the Outer Hebrides.

A ScotRail 153 Sprinter passing through the countryside near Connel Ferry on the Oban branch line.

Train enthusiasts will retrace their journeys back to Crianlarich to join the next train heading to Mallaig. The other possibility is to catch a bus to Fort William and rejoin the train there.

Highlights of the route from Crianlarich to Fort William are passing through the steep-sided Monessie Gorge, close to the River Spean, and the dramatic railway scenery in the country surrounding Ben Nevis, the highest mountain in the United Kingdom at 1,345 m (4,411 ft).

Fort William, one of the largest towns in the Highlands, situated at the southern end of the Great Glen, lies at the foot of Ben Nevis. It makes a wonderful base to discover the West Highlands, where scenes from the film *Local Hero* were shot. Fort William really is the base for outdoor activities such as hiking, loch cruising and biking, plus snow and water sports. Alternatively, relax at one of the several restaurants and bars lining Cameron Square.

From here, trains to Mallaig move along the track past mountainous landscapes that penetrate the clouds and lochs that shimmer in the sunlight. The extension of the route to Mallaig was built over a century ago with the intention of opening up the area and making the remote West Coast more accessible.

The Glenfinnan Viaduct, which was already well known before it featured in three *Harry Potter* films, is the most recognizable part of the whole journey. The viaduct, curving high over the River Finnan within sight of the waters of Loch Shiel, was built between 1897 and 1901. When it was completed, the expanse of 21 spans extending over 380 m (1,247 ft) was the largest concrete structure ever built. Its engineer, Robert McAlpine ('Concrete Bob'), was knighted for his achievement. The viaduct and a few other sites along the route have become pilgrimage locations for *Harry Potter* fans. The best views of the viaduct on the journey to Mallaig are from the rear and on the left-hand side of the train. The train often pauses on the viaduct if time permits to enable photography from it. The Glenfinnan Viaduct is also featured on a Bank of Scotland £10 banknote.

Just before its Mallaig terminus, the train crosses the River Morar, the United Kingdom's shortest river at just 1 km (3,281 ft) in length. Morar Station is also Britain's most westerly railway station. Mallaig overlooks Loch Nevis, Europe's deepest seawater loch. Mallaig was founded in the 1840s, and today is a busy fishing port and ferry terminal with services to Skye and the Small Isles. Attractions here include shops, bars, restaurants and, not surprisingly, an abundance of fish and chip shops.

ATTENTION TO DETAIL

The *Royal Scotsman* and *The Jacobite* are more luxurious than the regular service provided by ScotRail, but they are also more expensive. ScotRail operates six trains (Monday to Saturday but only three on Sunday) from Glasgow Queen Street terminus, with six trains to Oban and three through to Mallaig. Crianlarich is a key station where trains are divided for their respective services to either Oban or Mallaig.

Passengers who want to visit both Oban and Mallaig can travel from Glasgow to Oban via Crianlarich, then catch a bus to Fort William for the onward leg to Mallaig, or retrace their tracks from Oban to Crianlarich, for the onward journey to Mallaig. The first train from Glasgow to Oban departs at 5.20 a.m. and arrives at 8.35 a.m., stopping at 15 stations in between. The first train from Glasgow to Mallaig departs at 8.21 a.m. and arrives at 1.38 p.m. Passengers attempting to make a return journey in one day need to catch the return train from Mallaig at 4.05 p.m.; this arrives back into Glasgow at 9.25 p.m. It is far better to consider staying overnight in Oban, Fort William or Mallaig and rejoining a train the next day.

From Mallaig, CalMac ferries connect the mainland to the Isle of Skye. This peaceful coastal region appears about as remote as any destination in the world.

The Jacobite is a steam train that operates from Fort William to Mallaig twice daily from the start of May until the end of September. This award-winning train (voted 'Top Rail Journey

in the World' 2009–2013 by *Wanderlust Magazine*), is one of several services provided by the West Coast Railways. Passengers on *The Jacobite* travel in refurbished former British Rail carriages that date back to the 1950s. They can listen to a commentary on the main features along the route of 135 km (84 miles), while partaking of cream teas if so desired. Journeys to and from Fort William to Mallaig take 90 minutes. Seating in Standard Class and First Class is available, and passengers are advised to book well in advance for this popular tourist train. Return passengers have 90 minutes to explore the fishing village of Mallaig, including visiting Haggard Alley, the *Harry Potter* Shop.

HOGWARTS EXPRESS

As mentioned in one of the films, the *Hogwarts Express* is a 4-6-0 Hall Class steam locomotive, model number GWR 5900. *Hogwarts Express* was the name of the train that appeared in the *Harry Potter* films and operated from London King's Cross Station Platform 9¾ to the fictitious Hogsmeade Station. The train left Platform 9¾ without fail every 1 September at 11 a.m., arriving at Hogsmeade Station in the early evening.

Hogwarts Express made this journey six times a year, taking students to and from Hogwarts School of Witchcraft and Wizardry at the end or beginning of each term. Some students took the train back to King's Cross Station to go home for the Christmas and Easter holidays, but others stayed behind to spend their holidays at Hogwarts.

The actual front of the train used in the *Harry Potter* films as the *Hogwarts Express* is housed a long way away in Leavesden and can only be seen on a tour, 'The Making of *Harry Potter*', at the Warner Bros Studio. The Platform 9¾ section enables visitors to board the original carriages behind the steam locomotive used in the films. It is consistently acknowledged as one of the highest-rated attractions worldwide.

Opposite A four-car ScotRail 156 Sprinter crossing the famous Glenfinnan Viaduct.

Below *The Jacobite* headed by steam locomotives 44871 and 45407 climbing up to Glen Douglas from Arrochar.

FRANCE
TGV PARIS TO MARSEILLE

FRANCE'S RECORD-BREAKING TRAIN

France's high-speed train, Train à Grande Vitesse (TGV), operated by the Société Nationale des Chemins de fer Français (SNCF), services many of the nation's main cities and towns. Today, high-speed lines radiate from Paris to Lyon, Marseille, Bordeaux, Nantes, Strasbourg, Lille, Brussels and London, operating at their maximum speed on some routes. TGV trains additionally connect to Charles de Gaulle Airport in Paris and Lyon-Saint-Exupéry Airport. They also provide connectivity to popular tourist destinations such as Disneyland Paris, Brest, Avignon, Aix-en-Provence, Chambéry, Nice, Toulouse and Biarritz.

France is the long-time holder of the world speed record for conventional trains, set at an astonishing 574.8 km/h (357 mph) on 3 April 2007. However, this was only a test run, and France's

Opposite Le Train Bleu Restaurant, located in the hall of the Gare de Lyon in Paris, has featured in movies such as *Travels with my Aunt* (1972) and *Mr Bean's Holiday* (2002).

Below Passengers alighting from the Marseille to Paris TGV train at the Gare de Lyon in Paris.

upgraded over time. TGV inOui, SNCF premium TGV train services were introduced on certain high-speed rail routes in mid-2017. SNCF is currently replacing its 'classic' TGV services with the premium inOui and low-cost Ouigo services. The name 'inOui' is used as it resembles the French word 'inouï', meaning 'extraordinary' (more comfort, services and connectivity). By the end of 2018, TGV inOui trains were operating from Paris to Nice, Marseille and Lille, and were then introduced to the whole TGV network.

France has also exported this technology to several other countries, including South Korea, Spain, Taiwan, Morocco, Italy and the United States.

France's TGV network now carries some 110 million passengers annually. The high-speed line from Paris to Lyon is Europe's oldest and was extended to Marseille in 2001. The 188-minute service from Gare de Lyon Station in Paris to Marseille St Charles Station is an iconic TGV journey that links the capital with the famous Mediterranean Sea port.

TRACK NOTES

The high-speed line of 660 km (410 miles) between Paris and Marseille sees some 25 trains operate from 6 a.m. to 9 p.m. daily. These trains comprise a variety of single-deck and double-deck (Duplex) carriages. TGV trains reach their maximum speed of 320 km/h (199 mph) between Avignon and Aix-en-Provence on the way to Marseille.

TGV trains not only reduced travel times but also rapidly advanced train technology. For example, train drivers were unable to see and use conventional signalling due to the fact that TGV trains travelled so fast. In response, engineers developed Transmission Voie-Machine (TVM), or cab-signalling technology. Among other advances, this technology allows a train in an emergency braking situation to request, within seconds, that all following trains reduce their speed.

WELCOME ABOARD

The 'City of Light' is well worth several days' exploration before travelling south to Marseille. Paris is served by Europe's second-largest urban rail network, known as the Paris Métro. The Métro operates 16 lines and 308 stations, which are connected by 227 km (141 miles) of mostly underground track. The network carries more than four million commuters daily, with the station for the Marseille TGV accessible via Métro lines 1 and 14.

national network of TGV trains only operates at about half this speed, or 320 km/h (200 mph), on several lines. Europe's first dedicated high-speed network is still its best known and most successful.

The original idea, dating back to 1966, was for a network of turbotrains powered by gas turbines. However, an oil crisis in 1973 saw TGV prototypes evolve into electric trains. In 1976, SNCF placed an order with Alstom for 87 high-speed trains, and in 1981 the first TGV train entered service between Paris and Lyon. The Paris-centred network has been extended to most parts of the country, including Marseille, Bordeaux, Lille, Rennes, Strasbourg and Montpellier.

The original TGV trains of the 1980s have been replaced by more advanced, high-capacity Duplex double-decker trains capable of travelling beyond France into neighbouring countries including Spain, Belgium, Germany, Italy and Switzerland. The network to these countries uses a combination of high-speed and conventional track.

The TGV network has continually developed, improved and

An essential experience before departing Gare de Lyon is to dine at, or at least visit, the famous Train Bleu Restaurant within the station. It opened in 1903 with ornate Art Nouveau detailing. The restaurant opens in the late morning and remains open until 10.30 p.m., but its lounge bar opens at 7.30 a.m. and is popular for coffee, croissants, aperitifs and snacks.

The platforms at Gare de Lyon are always busy, but boarding the TGV train for Marseille is effortless. Seating in both classes on TGV trains is comfortable in the Christian Lacroix-designed interior.

Many TGV trains to Marseille are non-stop, while others make brief stops at a few places along the way. The main stops are Le Creusot Montceau, Lyon Part Dieu, Avignon and Aix-en-Provence. Most Marseille TGV services have double-decker carriages, with the upper level providing the best view. However, the lower floor is generally quieter, with fewer passengers moving through the carriages.

TGV trains pull into Marseille St Charles Station a little over three hours after departing Paris. The original station, built in 1848, has undergone several modernizations, with the last done to accommodate TGV trains. Numerous TGV services terminate or start their journey here, making St Charles the eleventh busiest railway station in France. The station provides a seamless interchange with the Marseille Métro.

The nation's second-largest city has a famous and somewhat notorious port, but a lot has changed through the revitalization of the city's older precincts. Life in the old days was portrayed in the 1971 action film *The French Connection*, which was shot around the port, the Old Town and other parts of southern France. It was one of the first R-rated films made, and the plot involved narcotics, smuggling, intrigue, assassination and inscrutable hit men.

The city's back alleys are still there, just a short tram ride from the station, but the port's dubious edginess has been replaced by smart new blocks of flats and hotels that dominate the city's best locations. Luxury yachts moor in the port, while daily pop-up fish markets offer fresh fish directly from trawlers moored along the docks. The dominant architectural feature on the eastern quay of the Old Port is the Vieux Port Pavilion, designed by Forster + Associates. This overhanging structure has a mirrored surface to create a unique perspective of the port. Other landmark structures

Left Marseille Saint-Charles is the city's main station for various railway services including TGV trains.

Opposite TGV trains from Paris Gare de Lyon to Marseille Saint-Charles cover the distance in three and a half hours.

include the impressive Cathédrale La Major, the old fort and MuCEM (the Museum of European and Mediterranean Civilizations).

ATTENTION TO DETAIL

All TGV trains are equipped with a cafe car, free Wi-Fi connectivity, power sockets and fold-down tables. Two classes of travel are available, first class and second class, and tickets can be bought several months in advance. Despite flexible pricing, tickets are generally less expensive the longer the booking period, and for travel outside peak times. Tickets can be bought online, at station ticket machines or counters, and need to be validated at an on-platform yellow machine just before departure. A reservation is compulsory and included in the fare, but is an additional charge for travel-pass holders. Trains to and from Marseille depart Paris at hourly intervals.

First-class passengers benefit from wide seats, some solo seats and a separate lounge for up to eight passengers. Passengers who book a First Class Business Première ticket receive additional benefits during their travels. They can expect complimentary snacks and drinks, access to the Grand Voyageur Lounge, and exclusive content on the TGV multimedia portal. Lounge access is provided at Gare de Lyon and Marseille Stations.

Lille is a key station, especially for travellers who choose to travel from London on Eurostar services. A TGV service that bypasses Paris operates directly from Lille to Marseille. In Marseille a change of train is required for those who wish to continue on the TGV to Nice. This rail journey from London to Marseille, using a combination of Eurostar and TGV, takes seven hours and 40 minutes.

It is also possible to travel on regional trains along the original rail route and stop for sightseeing at stations along the way. The Trains Express Régionaux (TER) route to Marseille stops at Dijon, Beaune, Lyon, Orange, Avignon and Arles, and takes nine hours. TER trains vary in size and carriage composition, but are typically modern, single-deck, diesel-hauled units with no cafe car. Ticket prices on these local and regional trains are more affordable than on TGV, and tickets are best bought on the day as prices are fixed with no early purchase discounts. Separate tickets from Paris to Lyon and Lyon to Marseille need to be purchased. There are also no seat reservations, but space is allocated for luggage and bikes (there is no charge for a bike on TER trains, but there is a small surcharge on TGV services).

MONT BLANC EXPRESS

ONE MOUNTAIN, THREE TRAINS

Chamonix made headlines when it hosted the first Winter Olympics in 1924. Even before then, cross-country skiers were aware of its challenging terrain, and mountaineers knew of the thrill of climbing Mont Blanc (4,808 m / 15,773 ft). Most travellers start this scenic journey in Martigny in Valais Canton in Switzerland's far south. The route crosses the border into eastern France and continues through the Chamonix Valley under the Col des Montets, to Argentiere and Chamonix, then to St Gervais/Le Fayet. From here, trains on the French SNCF network connect to Lyon and Paris.

The Mont-Blanc Tramway and the Montenvers and Mer de Glace Train operate near the main line, making this an essential region for train enthusiasts to visit.

TRACK NOTES

In Switzerland, the express is known as the Martigny to Châtelard Railway, and beyond Châtelard-Frontière in France it becomes the St Gervais to Vallorcine Railway. It extends along 38 km (23.6 miles) of track (18 km / 11.2 miles in Switzerland and 20 km / 12.4 miles in France), and takes 90 minutes to reach Chamonix and

another 45 minutes to reach the St Gervais terminus. Two-car Z800 units with seating for 105 passengers operate on narrow-gauge electrified lines using rack-and-pinion traction.

WELCOME ABOARD

This journey begins in Martigny and proceeds south-west into Chamonix, a French alpine resort located in the Alps. Trains from Switzerland's south-west (Geneva, Lausanne and Montreux) or north-east (Zurich, Lucerne, Chur and Brig) pass through Martigny, where passengers need to alight for the *Mont Blanc Express* into the French Alps.

The route initially travels along a gently inclining line before crossing the River Trient, a tributary of the River Rhône. Trains reach the Trient Gorge, crossing the wild, rocky canyon using a series of bridges. They pass vineyards where grapes are sourced to produce Chasselas wine (known as Fendant in Valais). The track closely follows the River Trient before crossing the French border, with glimpses of Mont Blanc, France's highest mountain, first appearing.

Vallorcine is the first stop in France where it is possible to access the Tour-Balme area. Visitors who want to visit Emosson Dam can alight at Le Chatelard VS Station. Several stops provide access to cable cars and lifts for the many ski fields. These include Montroc for the Tour-Balme cable car, and Le Buet, where La Poya lift is also popular.

After its final ascent along one of the line's steepest sections, the train arrives in Chamonix. This is the valley's largest and most frequented station, providing access to the Aiguille du Midi, the Montenvers train and the Brevent cable car. Chamonix is a popular year-round destination with its stunning mountain panoramas.

ATTENTION TO DETAIL

Trains operate from the early morning until late evening. For those staying in the Chamonix Valley, journeys on the *Mont Blanc Express* are free with the Carte d'Hote, which is distributed by hotels. It provides complimentary access to all public transport from Servoz to Vallorcine. The express is not included in the Swiss Travel Pass.

Opposite Transports de Martigny et Régions (TMS) is a Swiss-owned company that operates some rail and bus services in the Mont Blanc region.

Below The winter scenery around Mont Blanc is especially appealing.

MONT-BLANC TRAMWAY

The Mont-Blanc Tramway (Tramway du Mont Blanc) is an electrified mountain railway that ascends from St-Gervais-les-Bains to the Nid d'Aigle (Eagle's Nest) terminus at 2,362 m (7,749 ft). This makes it France's highest railway. It is popular, especially with climbers heading towards the main climbing route to Mont Blanc. This journey provides travellers with wonderful views of the Bionnassay Glacier, Mont Lachat and Prarion. Due to the possibility of avalanches, winter trains terminate at Bellevue Station. The line for this rack and adhesion railway is 12.4 km (7.7 miles) long with a 1,000 mm (3 ft 3⅜ in) gauge. It operates at an average gradient of 15 per cent and a maximum gradient of 24 per cent.

Montenvers Train & Mer de Glace
The Chemin de fer du Montenvers cogwheel train to Montenvers departs from its dedicated station next to Chamonix main station. This funicular climbs steeply to a scenic location above Mer de Glace to provide views of Les Drus and Les Grandes Jorasses. Visitors can walk to the glacier from Montenvers top station at an altitude of 1,913 m (6,276 ft). In summer there are numerous walking trails down the valley and traverses along the mountains to Plan de l'Aiguille. The line of 5.1 km (3.2 miles) has the same gauge as the Mont-Blanc Tramway. It too operates using rack and adhesion technology along gradients of up to 22 per cent.

CHEMINS DE FER DE LA CORSE

SCENIC MEDITERRANEAN ISLAND JOURNEYS

The mountainous French island of Corsica in the Tyrrhenian Sea is closer to Italy than France and benefits from both cultures. Corsica, covering 8,722 km² (3,368 mi²), is 183 km (114 miles) long and 82 km (51 miles) wide. The island is located immediately north of Sardinia across the Strait of Bonifacio, and there are ferry services between the two. Both Sardinia and Corsica have extensive railway networks, with the latter operated by Chemins de Fer de la Corse (CFC). The first railway opened on the island in 1888, and its operations are now based in Ponte Leccia in the northern middle part of the island. This is the main junction for train lines heading roughly north–south and east–west. An east coast line that was badly damaged in the Second World War has closed.

There have been several attempts to close the whole network or sections of it, but it remains open to provide a wonderful way to explore many parts of the island.

TRACK NOTES

Corsica has 232 km (144 miles) of mostly single-line track. Visitors can travel on the entire system by arriving in Calvi, then travelling to Ponte Leccia, on to Bastia, then retracing the line back to Ponte Leccia before heading south-west to the terminus at Ajaccio. Corsica has a metre-wide gauge rail network.

The network's longest tunnel, located near Vizzavona, is 4 km (2.4 miles) long. At an altitude of 906 m (2,972 ft), it is also the highest point of the railway. A viaduct on the line over the River Vecchio located between Venaco and Vivario has been incorrectly atributed to Gustave Eiffel, known for the tower named after him in Paris. The viaduct is 140 m (459 ft) long and 94 m (308 ft) high.

WELCOME ABOARD

A railway operates from north to south, connecting Bastia with Ajaccio, and east to west, from Ponte Leccia to Calvi. Three main lines operate – Bastia to Ajaccio, Ajaccio to Calvi, and Bastia to Calvi. The local Balagne Line, from Calvi to L'Île-Rousse and back, skirts many beaches and is highly recommended. It passes through 14 stations on a one-way journey of 24 km (15 miles), taking about an hour.

The Calvi and Balagne areas are two of the most visited parts of Corsica. Balagne showcases rugged landscapes, quaint French towns and numerous untouched beaches. Its beaches make it a popular summer resort destination. Calvi is best known for its architecture from the Roman era, and its cobbled streets are lined with harbourside cafes and colourful houses.

Seaside Bastia in the north-east dates back to the Roman era. It is one of France's busiest ports and the northern terminus for the train to Ajaccio via Ponte Leccia. Suburban trains operate from here to Casamozza.

The Regional National Park of Corsica in the island's mountainous interior was opened in 1972 to protect flora and fauna, including two endangered species: the Mouflon (a wild sheep) and the Corsican Red Deer.

Corsica is noted for wines made from the Sciacarello and Nielluccio (red) and Vermentino (white) grape varieties. The island's nine wine regions are extensive but mostly located around the coasts, with some wineries in Calvi, south of Bastia and Ajaccio, accessible by train.

Corte, the former Corsican capital (7,500 residents), has a fortress and a fascinating old town with a citadel dating back to 1419.

The north–south train terminates in Ajaccio in the island's south-west. Napoleon Bonaparte was born here in 1769, and the family home is now a museum. The Napoleon Trail starts in Ajaccio, while the gruelling GR20 walk of 180 km (112 miles) from Calenzana to Conca is best left to experienced trekkers.

Despite the name, Eiffel Viaduct, which crosses the Vecchio River, is wrongly attributed to Gustave Eiffel, but riding a train over it is a highlight of a Corsican rail journey.

ATTENTION TO DETAIL

Travellers can arrive in Corsica at the main ports of L'Île Rousse, Bastia, Ajaccio and Porto-Vecchio by ferry from Marseille, Toulon and Nice (France), or Italian ports such as Genoa, Savona and Livorno. The ports of Calvi and Bastia are serviced by trains. Corsica is best avoided during the European summer holidays, especially in July and August, when trains are crowded. A seven-day pass provides access to all public transport on the island, while senior residents, children and the disabled receive generous discounts.

RAUMA LINE

FROM FJORDS TO MOUNTAINS

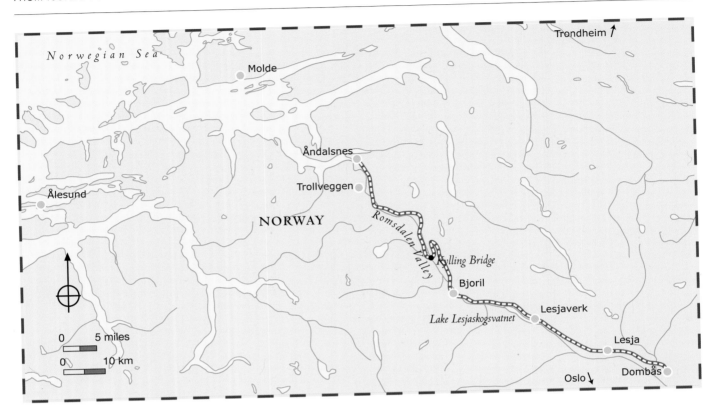

This scenic Norwegian line begins in Dombås and passes through picturesque mountains, across impressive bridges and through winding tunnels before ending in Åndalsnes on Isfjorden, a branch of the mighty Romsdal Fjord. The Rauma Line (Raumabanen) of 114 km (71 miles), running down the Romsdalen Valley, has been referred to as 'one of Norway's most beautiful and wildest railway lines'.

The Norwegian Parliament approved building the railway in 1908, with construction beginning in 1912. It opened in three stages between 1921 and 1924 as a branch of the Dovre Line (Oslo to Trondheim). It was originally intended to connect Ålesund, Molde and Kristiansund, but this did not happen.

Only five railway stations remain in use along the line: Dombås, Lesja, Lesjaverk, Bjorli and Åndalsnes. The service is operated by SJ Nord, and the line mostly serves as a feeder service for express trains on the Dovre Line. The introduction of a high-speed railway on the Rauma Line is being debated.

TRACK NOTES

Steam locomotives hauling passenger trains ceased on the line in 1958. In 2000, two-car Class 93 Diesel Multiple Units (DMU) were introduced on the four daily services in each direction on the Rauma Line. The night-train service has been terminated and replaced by an express bus. In summer, tourist trains often carry passengers arriving in Åndalsnes on cruise ships. These trains spend more time in Dombås to enable tourists to explore its attractions. A steam train is also used for special occasions on this route.

WELCOME ABOARD

The train, with its panoramic windows, air conditioning and comfortable seating, is well equipped to accommodate tourists. Maps and guides on some trains also enhance the passenger experience. The train has disabled facilities and a toilet.

Dombås is nothing more than a village, although there is accommodation in a hotel and the church appeals to some visitors. Interestingly, the first American military casualty of the Second

Dombås Station is one of the terminus stations for regional trains that operate on the Rauma Line.

World War died in the town in 1940. Captain Robert Losey, who was serving as an air attaché to American embassies in the Nordic countries, was killed here along with five Norwegians during a German bombing attack. There is a memorial in the town.

Just beyond Dombås Station (Stasjon), the line splits with the Rauma Line heading westwards from the town and crosses the Jora Bridge, which is 37 m (121 ft) in length. It passes through the valley with high mountains on either side, including the Dovrefjell-Sunndalsfjella National Park on the right-hand side. The train stops at the village of Lesja, which serves the farming community here. The national park appeals to summer hikers, while in winter it is favoured by skiers. However, due to its terrain, isolation and long walks, outdoor activities are best left to experienced hikers. The mountains of the national park are featured in a scene from the *Harry Potter* film *Harry Potter and the Half-Blood Prince* (2009).

The next stop is Lesjaverk, beside Lake Lesjaskogsvatnet. The train follows the lake, with the best view to be had from the left-hand side of the train. The elongated lake is interesting in that it is fed by two rivers, the Gudbransdalslågen and Rauma. During the Second World War, RAF 263 Squadron, which flew 'Gloster Gladiators', was briefly based here in 1940 and used the frozen lake for taking off and landing.

Bjorli is the next stop and is popular in the winter with skiers as it is one of Norway's many reliable ski centres, with ski lifts, alpine courses and cross-country skiing in the forested mountains. It receives early snow, and its chairlift covers ski fields extending

down a vertical drop of 660 m (2,170 ft) and many cross-country ski trails. In summer, the village is a base for mountaineering expeditions and horse riding, plus river activities like fishing and canoeing.

From here, the already enchanting journey becomes more exhilarating. This is where the adventurous, steep and incredibly beautiful sections of the track begin. The journey also becomes more fascinating for rail enthusiasts – because the steep terrain through which the train passes presented a problem to the engineers due to altitude differences between the top and bottom of the valley. The solution was to build two turning tunnels with a double loop at Verma. The train entering the Stavem Tunnel begins at 332 m (1,089 ft) above sea level and travels through the 1,396 m (4,580 ft) tunnel. It makes a horseshoe turn in the tunnel and leaves it in the opposite direction. The views of the Romsdalen Valley at the exit are worth the wait.

Then the railway goes into the 480 m (1,575 ft) Kylling Tunnel, where the train turns again. The train exits on to the 77 m (253 ft) Kylling Bridge, Norway's most famous railway bridge. Perched 60 m (197 ft) above the River Rauma, the view down the Vermafossen Canyon, with its waterfall that drops 850 m (2,789 ft), is one of the many picturesque sights along the line.

The scenery that follows is spectacularly wild, including mountains like Trollveggen, Europe's tallest rock face, which towers 1,000 m (3,281 ft) vertically on the left-hand side of the train. The Romsdalshorn, Karlskråtind, Mongeura and Vengetindene follow.

Flowing down from them are notable waterfalls such as Brudesløret, Gravdefossen and Mongefossen.

Before arriving at Åndalsnes Station, the train passes Mount Nesaksla (715 m/2,356 ft). There are bus services between Åndalsnes and Kristiansund, Ålesund or Molde, from where it is possible to explore more of coastal Norway.

From the station, visitors can walk directly to the Romsdal Gondola for the ascent to Mount Nesaksla for impressive views up the Romsdalen Valley and down to the Romsdalsfjord. Åndalsnes is an adventure capital for climbing, hiking and various winter sports. Although it is just a town of 2,500 residents, it is popular and well set up for tourism, especially cruise ships. Energetic visitors can hike the famous Romsdalseggen Ridge, go ski touring or experience the Norwegian Scenic Route Geiranger-Trollstigen.

ATTENTION TO DETAIL

Passengers initially have to travel from Oslo to Dombås, located 343 km (213 miles) north of the capital Oslo, on the Dovre Line to Trondheim. There are some six daily departures on Vy to Dombås, with journeys taking between three and four and a half hours, the first departure from Oslo being at 8.02 a.m. and the last at 11.06 p.m. The first departure from Dombås to Oslo is at 2.26 a.m. and the last at 6.10 p.m.

The Rauma Line runs throughout the year but only provides seating in second-class carriages, and the journey takes some 85 minutes. The first train from Dombås to Åndalsnes departs at 12.08 p.m. with the last at 8.16 p.m., while trains operating in the reverse direction, from Åndalsnes to Dombås, start at 7.10 a.m., with the last departure being at 4.30 p.m. For those with limited time, it is possible to leave Oslo on the first train to Dombås for the immediate connection on the Rauma Line. This train arrives in Åndalsnes at 1.28 p.m. The return journey departs Åndalsnes at 4.30 p.m. and travels back to Dombås for the connecting train to Oslo, which leaves at 6.10 p.m. This train arrives in the capital at 10.02 p.m. An overnight stay or longer is recommended, as there is so much to admire along the Rauma Line and in Åndalsnes,

A high-speed railway between Ålesund and Oslo via Romsdalen is planned. This line would connect at Dombås to a proposed high-speed line between Oslo and Trondheim, but would avoid going through Åndalsnes. This will pass through the village of Bjorli and through the Valldalen Valley, before reaching the village of Valldal in Sunnmøre. The branch line would be 193 km (120 miles) long, of which 89 km (55 miles) would run through tunnels and 13 km (8 miles) over bridges and viaducts.

A journey with Rauma Railway is wild and beautiful, regardless of the season of travel. However, during the summer, a tourist service operates from Åndalsnes to Bjorli only.

SWEDEN
THE INLANDSBANAN

A SLOW JOURNEY TO THE ARCTIC CIRCLE

The Inlandsbanan is a Swedish railway that operates in summer (from mid-June to late August) and covers a distance of 1,300 km (807 miles) from Kristinehamn northwards to Gällivare in Lapland. A continuous journey on this route would take two days, but extended tours are available. The line was built between 1908 and 1937 mainly to gain access to valuable natural resources such as timber and minerals. It was also thought to be strategically important to have a line that connected the northern and southern parts of the country. Traffic along the line was always light and unprofitable and remained dormant for some years after SJ (Swedish Railway) abandoned the line. Various sections of the line are now managed by the municipalities along the route.

Beyond Gällivare, the railway crosses the Arctic Circle at Kiruna before continuing on to Narvik in the far north of

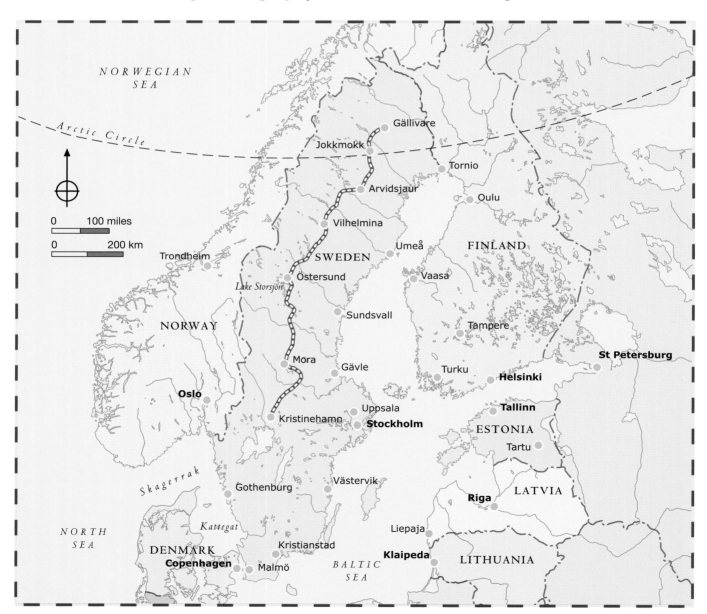

neighbouring Norway. A western loop is possible by continuing south through Norway, then returning from Trondheim (Norway) to Östersund (Sweden). An easterly loop, back from Gällivare and entirely through Sweden, passes through Umeå, Sundsvall and Uppsala before reaching its Stockholm terminus. Joining the train in Mora may be more convenient for visitors who arrive in Sweden via Stockholm.

Some travellers mention long sections of forest with few distractions, which may not be so appealing to casual train fans. However, the opportunity to witness the midnight sun (June to early July), adds to the journey's enjoyment.

TRACK NOTES

The railway operates on standard-gauge track and uses Y1 diesel-hydraulic, two-car railcars. These provide reasonably comfortable seating of four seats across a central aisle, with some clusters of four seats with a table between. These trains date back to the 1970s, with few modern facilities apart from a toilet. Occasionally, special steam-locomotive excursions are also available.

WELCOME ABOARD

The train provides an opportunity for passengers to experience the Swedish countryside by alighting at some of the 70 stops along the way. It slows down in photogenic areas to allow passengers to take photos. This is not a journey for those who want to reach a destination in a hurry. Passengers with mobility problems should think seriously about travelling on the train. The charm of travelling by train, back to a bygone era, is enhanced by the fact that train timetables are not always strictly followed.

Tours are available along the way to break up the journey and take in the key locations along the route. Passengers travelling northwards would typically stay overnight in Mora, Östersund, Vilhelmina, Jokkmokk and Gällivare.

Regular SJ trains from Gothenburg, Stockholm and several other Swedish cities connect to the terminus stations of Mora, Östersund and Gällivare.

Right Endless pine forests dominate the scenery along the route.

Opposite The train passes a Swedish landscape characterized by many lakes, which are the result of glacial erosion.

Passengers can travel on a special summer service from Kristinehamn to Mora. The original *Inlandsbanan* line started in Kristinehamn, but this has now been abandoned. However, in summer, passengers can travel between both towns via another railway line, with the distance being 297 km (178 miles) and the journey taking about six and a half hours.

Mora is a small town located between Siljan and Orsasjön Lake and is now considered the southern terminus of *Inlandsbanan*. The journey from Mora to Östersund takes five and a half hours (321 km/199 miles). The train from Mora to Östersund travels through the town of Sveg. On arrival, passengers can stop in Sveg and at the Tandsjö or Fågelsjö Lakes.

The train passes through wilderness forests of birch and pine on its journey from Mora to Östersund. The latter is scenically located on the foreshore of Lake Storsjön ('Great Lake'). There are tens of thousands of lakes in Sweden, but this is one of the largest. Östersund, with a population of 50,000, is best known as a winter sports destination, but it is also picturesque in summer. Its Jamtli Outdoor Museum is located in a historical setting. The city is an important transport hub, with train connections to Stockholm and Trondheim.

Trains from Östersund to Vilhelmina enter Lapland (Laponia). Two outstanding landmarks in Vilhelmina are the Hembygdsmuseet Museum and the old church village of Kyrkstad. The Laponian Area is a vast mountainous wilderness in northern Sweden. Covering 9,400 km^2 (3,600 mi^2), it is regarded as the world's largest unmodified nature area to be still cultured by an indigenous population. Here, the Saami (Sami) people herd Reindeer and follow annual migration paths. The UNESCO World Heritage Site comprises two nature reserves and four national parks.

The train travels past Moskosel, with its Navvy Museum (Rallarmuséet) located in the old railway station building. This museum celebrates the hard-working navvys who laboured to lay the rail tracks under harsh conditions. Another museum, the *Inlandsbanan* Museum, located in the freight shed at Sorsele, provides detailed information on the history of the inland railway. Stories about those who built the railway and those who fought to keep it open are interesting. In, Gasa to the east, the Båtsuoj Sami Centre provides an insight into Reindeer.

The train stops just south of Jokkmokk at Gografiska Polcirkeln Station located on the Arctic Circle at (66° 33' N). Tin handicrafts are available in Jokkmokk, and the Sami Museum is well worth visiting, as is an alpine garden that highlights the importance of local medicinal herbs.

From Jokkmokk, the train takes 90 minutes to reach Gällivare. At the right time of the year, an evening walk along the river may reveal the midnight sun on a clear evening.

The train passes through forests that are home to Sweden's four big predators: the Wolf, Bear, Lynx and Wolverine. There is an abundance of Reindeer and Elk, and beautiful birds of prey to be seen from the tracks. Despite the best efforts of the driver, sadly some of these animals collide with the train on its journey.

The train provides a toilet, windows that open, Wi-Fi and USB ports, but being an old train, it is not well equipped to accommodate passengers with mobility issues.

ATTENTION TO DETAIL

The railway operates daily departures from mid-June until the end of August. At other times of the year, the entire train can be booked for charter journeys. The stretch between Kristinehamn and Mora is open during the high season (summer), with the journey completed in collaboration with Tågab, another train company operating along this route.

Hot beverages and snacks are served on the train, while it also stops for more substantive meals at suitable stations (passengers order in advance via the train host, so their meal is ready on arrival at the respective stations). Some stations provide a service for takeaway meals and beverages. These trains are mostly staffed by knowledgeable train hosts who pass on information in Swedish and English to passengers on their journey. Track commentary brochures are also available. Seat reservations for groups are compulsory and recommended for individuals.

Inlandsbanan Cards are available for hop-on/hop-off travel in the summer, but passengers still need to make seat reservations. The pass card enables two weeks of unlimited travel and enables passengers to stop and make detours from the train line along the way. Up to two children aged below 15 travel free when accompanied by an adult, while young people aged 16–25 receive 25 per cent discounts.

Various train tours are available, including 'Discover the Inlandsbanan'. Another, the Wilderness Train (Vildmarkståget), departs Stockholm for an eight-day journey that takes a round trip via Östersund and Inlandsbanan up to Gällivare, then via Malmbanan to Narvik in Norway. This historic train journey is done in collaboration with the Railway Museum in Gävle. The train consists of restored heritage first-class carriages of the 40s, 50s and 60s and a restaurant carriage, hauled by various locomotives, including steam ones, on different routes.

During the winter, a night train runs from Malmö to Östersund and Röjan via Stockholm to serve the Vemdalen Ski Resort.

FINLAND
SANTA CLAUS EXPRESS

HELSINKI TO ROVANIEMI

While there are several regular daily services from Helsinki to the Arctic Circle destination of Rovaniemi, the most unique train is the *Santa Claus Express*. This train travels to Rovaniemi, which is the gateway to Lapland and is promoted as the home of Santa Claus. Not only is the train named after Father Christmas, but it also has a giant sticker of Santa Claus on its white and red livery. Naturally, the service is very popular with children and families, and those living out their own 'polar express' fantasies.

The double-decker night trains connect the Finnish capital to Rovaniemi, and from there, one of these trains continues on to Kemijärvi, a little over an hour away to the north-east. The line, and a more north-westerly route from Kemi to Kolari, cross the Arctic Circle at 66.6° N. It is possible to have your photo taken with one foot on either side of this imaginary line.

Alternatively, passengers can travel on the Rovaniemi route at other times of the day for a very different experience from the night train. In summer, it is possible to admire the midnight sun, while a winter journey provides an opportunity to witness the famous Northern Lights. Travel in the summer is ideal for passengers since they can gaze out of the panoramic train windows and admire the passing countryside.

Train services are operated by Finnish Rail (VR) and take between eight and a half and 12 hours to reach Santa's homeland. Rovaniemi, the Lapland capital, was connected to the rail network via Kemi in 1909. Freight and passenger trains once continued from Rovaniemi to Kemijärvi and Salla in eastern Lapland, near the Russian border. However, the section between Isokylä and Salla was closed in December 2012. There have been discussions about establishing a multi-nation Arctic railway, reopening this section of the line, and continuing it across the border to Kandalaksha and Murmansk in northwestern Russia. The development of the concept has stalled due to regional geopolitics and concerns about the line's commercial viability.

TRACK NOTES

This Finnish train is one of Northern Europe's most comfortable and exciting trains. The train is clean and comfortable, and it travels very smoothly along the track. Its carriage interiors are decorated in white and green along sleek, curved wall corridors.

The line is electrified all the way to Kemijärvi, and Swiss Sr2 electric locomotives haul the trains. German Sr3 electric locomotives are commonly used on this passenger service. Trains on the route travel at a maximum speed of 140 km/h (90 mph), although they can travel at faster speeds. French rolling stock company Alstom has supplied VR with Sm3 trains, which operate from Helsinki to Turku, Tampere, Jyväskylä, Oulu, Kouvola, Joensuu and Vaasa. Trains heading north from Kemi to Kolari are typically worked by VR Dr16 Class or the smaller Dv12 Class diesel locomotives.

WELCOME ABOARD

Trains depart from Helsinki Central Station (Helsingin päärautatieasema) and stop at Tampere, Oulu and Rovaniemi. Currently a few trains per week continue on to Kemijärvi. Helsinki Central is one of the most famous and distinctive railway stations in the world (in 2013 the BBC declared it one of the world's most beautiful railway stations). The granite-clad edifice was designed by Eliel Saarinen, one of Finland's foremost architects and urban planners. It was built between 1905 and 1919 and served as an

Christmas falls every day of the year at Santa Claus Village in Rovaniemi.

inspiration for the Singapore Railway Station. The station is a hub for the city's commuter rail network and long-distance trains, as well as being connected to the international airport. Its concourse is impressive and provides access to 19 platforms beneath a high and expansive iron and glass roof. It has excellent facilities, including shops where passengers can stock up on snacks and beverages before the long haul to Rovaniemi.

The train's first major stop is Tampere, where the train from Turku in Finland's south-west is connected to the service from Helsinki. Both Tampere and Turku are 190 km (120 miles) or 90 minutes by train from Helsinki. With a population of 342,000, Tampere is Finland's second-largest urban area and an important transport hub, with some 150 trains passing through Tampere Central Railway Station each day.

Some 483 km (300 miles) into the trip, the train reaches Kokkola on the Gulf of Bothnia and the northernmost reaches of the Baltic Sea. The landscape is flat and dissected by rivers. While most of its 50,000 residents speak Finnish, some speak Swedish.

The seaside resort of Oulu, with some 205,000 residents, is the next major stop for the train. Located at the mouth of the River Oulujoki, which flows into the Gulf of Bothnia, Oulu began as an ancient trading port. Finland's fifth-largest city, with the nation's second-busiest airport, is situated 680 km (420 miles) north of Helsinki. Oulu has been chosen as the European Capital of Culture for 2026; it also stages the Air Guitar Championship every August.

Above Passengers travelling on the Santa Claus Express board the train at Helsinki Central Railway Station.

Left Helsinki Central Station combines Renaissance Revival and Gothic Revival architectural styles, a common practice for other European railway stations built in the early 20th century.

The train continues north to the town of Kemi, located 105 km (65 miles) from Oulu. While the town is small, with just 20,000 residents, it is an important railway junction for trains to Kolari and Rovaniemi. Kemi is located at the northern end of the Gulf of Bothnia, close to the Swedish town of Haparanda. Some travellers may be distracted here by the world's largest snow castle, and associated attractions such as the SnowHotel, SnowRestaurant, SnowChapel and an adventure park for children. The town is especially popular with skiers passing on their way to skiing fields and resorts located further to the north.

From Kemi, the train travels another 117 km (73 miles) to reach Rovaniemi, located at the confluence of two rivers and bordered on three sides by water. It is home not only to Santa Claus, but also to 64,000 citizens, some of whom act as Santa's

The *Santa Claus Express* passes through Lapland and the Arctic Circle before terminating in Rovaniemi.

helpers and operate reindeer-powered sleighs to transport excited visitors. Numerous activities to suit all ages are available in Rovaniemi. The Santa Claus Village is situated just a few kilometres from the city centre, and a bus service operates from the railway station. The city was almost razed to the ground by the Germans in 1944, and a new plan, in the shape of reindeer antlers, was conceived by Alvar Aalto, one of Finland's leading architects.

Every day is Christmas in Rovaniemi, as Santa Claus makes regular appearances in town, and the post office receives mail from children around the globe. Snow covers the ground for half the year (late November to early May), and winter temperatures drop below zero, with the coldest day recorded at -45°C. Of course, this is perfect for those seeking the finest setting for Christmas celebrations.

Rovaniemi is also a gateway to many other destinations and activities in Lapland. Visitors can take a husky or reindeer sleigh ride, see reindeer in the wild or take a short walk through sections of Lapland's forests. Traditional dishes served in restaurants in this part of Finland include salmon, reindeer and elk meat.

Arktikum houses the University of Lapland's Arctic Science Centre and the Regional Museum of Lapland. It has information on the Sami, who are the indigenous and formerly nomadic people of the north. They are the original inhabitants of Lapland who were once commonly known as Lapps. The centre features many other topics such as the history of the region, Arctic nature and the science behind the Northern Lights.

The area is also an excellent location for sighting the Northern Lights, or 'Revontulet', as they are known in Finland. This amazing light phenomenon is caused by electrically charged solar particles colliding with atmospheric gases above the Magnetic Pole. The autumn and late winter are the best times to see the Northern Lights. The recommended months are the end of March or the end of September. However, it is worth noting that many days are cloudy due to falling snow, and that this is an opportunistic event that is dependent on solar activity. It helps to join a tour, as

experienced guides know the best locations to witness what the scientific community calls the 'aurora borealis'.

Many travellers to Finland are attracted by the opportunity to witness the Northern lights at places like Lake Inari near Nanguniemi.

ATTENTION TO DETAIL

There are six trains per day between Helsinki Central Station and Rovaniemi. The four day trains each take about eight hours to cover the route of 880 km (547 miles), while the two night trains take 12 hours and 42 minutes to reach their destination (these trains make multiple stops along the route). The first train from Rovaniemi departs at 5.27 a.m., while the last leaves at 8.57 p.m. From Helsinki, the overnight departures leave at 7.29 p.m. (arriving in Rovaniemi at 7.29 a.m. the next morning), and 11.13 p.m. (arriving in Rovaniemi at 11.13 a.m. the next morning). Overnight trains from Rovaniemi to Helsinki depart at 5.45 p.m. and arrive in Helsinki at 6.27 a.m. the next morning, and at 5.45 p.m., arriving in Helsinki the next morning at 9.27 a.m.

Passengers do not have to travel on the night train as there are several departures during the day. These trains cover the distance much more quickly than the night train, and while they do not provide sleeping compartments, they give an opportunity to admire the passing countryside.

Naturally, the train is especially popular in December, and seat reservations are mandatory for this month and all other departures. Tickets are also more expensive this month due to the high demand. December-departure reservations are best made online well in advance. Saver tickets are available for those who do book well in advance, but once these are sold, passengers have to pay the full price. The train is one of the most affordable ways to travel to Lapland, as overnight travellers save on the cost of an expensive hotel.

There are several seating and sleeping options, from a seat to a deluxe sleeper, with or without a private bathroom. Seating cars include a service table, power sockets, Wi-Fi and a reading light.

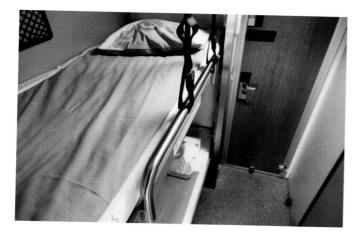

Left Comfortable bunk-style sleeping is provided on the train on its journey to the Arctic Circle. Cabins are like a small hotel room on rails with duvets, pillows and sheets provided in sleeper cabins and bath towels for cabins with an attached shower.

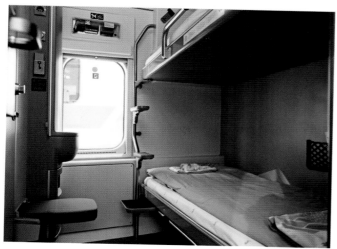

The seating is arranged in three rows, with the opportunity to select a single seat if desired, and the seats have a slight recline. There are chargeable compartments for large bags, bikes and skis, while pet transportation can be arranged for an additional fee. Some carriages also have an accessible toilet that can accommodate passengers confined to a wheelchair. The lights in the seating carriages remain on all night, so light sleepers may want to bring an eye mask if they plan to rest on the long journey.

Passengers who book a sleeper cabin have the choice of an upstairs or downstairs berth. Both are fitted out with bunk beds (one upper and one lower) for two people. Pillows, sheets, duvets and towels are supplied to those in cabins with en-suite bathrooms; pillows, sheets and duvets are provided for those in lower deck compartments. Upstairs compartments cost more but are equipped with an en-suite bathroom (washbasin, shower and toilet). Block-out curtains are installed, and alarm clocks ensure that passengers will not oversleep. Doors lock automatically, but a key card is

available for those who want to leave their compartment and walk around the train.

Those travelling in downstairs cabins have access to communal restrooms in each carriage (access to the facilities is via a keycard, which is made available in each cabin). Families can book two adjoining downstairs cabins with a door that can be opened between the two cabins. Children aged 10 and younger are able to travel for free if staying in a compartment with their parents (a ticket needs to be issued even though it is 'free'). However, space is limited, and passengers with large bags should consider booking these into the baggage car. This service is chargeable except for baby strollers, which can also be stored here.

The *Santa Claus Express* makes a long journey, and it is advisable to wear comfortable clothing and/or take pyjamas. While the outside weather is below freezing point in winter, the train's interior is fully air conditioned and sufficiently warm. Each sleeping compartment has an adjustable thermostat.

There is a single-level restaurant/bistro car where snacks, hot meals and beverages are served. Stool seating facing the window is available, as are standing areas in the centre of the restaurant car. The menu features dishes like pasta, meatballs and sandwiches, while all-day breakfast is also available from a compact menu that includes warm beverages. Passengers can also take their own food and drinks on the train. Meals can also be ordered in advance and delivered to the cabins by the conductor.

Pet and car owners will appreciate the train's policy of allowing both animals and vehicles on board, at an extra cost. Car-carrier wagons are available on most services and loading time begins about 90 minutes before the train departs.

Trains for Rovaniemi also depart from Turku and join the main line north at Tampere. International trains from Helsinki once proceeded into Russia for St Petersburg and Moscow, but these have been cancelled indefinitely.

BERNINA EXPRESS

RHAETIAN RHAPSODY

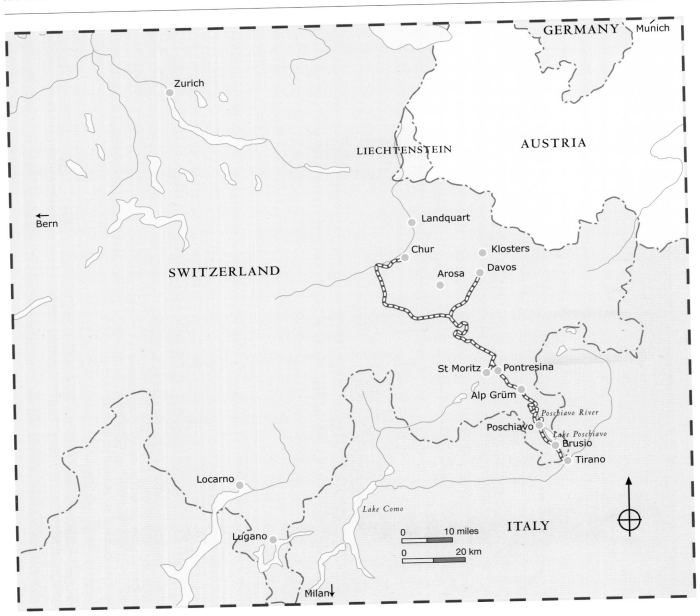

The *Bernina Express* travels from Alpine Switzerland to northern Italy through a setting very reminiscent of the Mediterranean. The journey of 163 km (101 miles) takes five hours and extends from Tirano in northern Italy through eastern Switzerland, past St Moritz and on to Landquart. The railway traverses the Rhaetian Alps and the Engadin Valley, and its construction was a major engineering feat recognized by UNESCO in 2008 for its world heritage. As such, it is one of just a few global railways to be so inscribed (the Semmeringbahn or Semmering Railway, page 119, is another).

The route traverses alpine forests, incised valleys, glaciers, lakes and thundering waterfalls. While the journey only takes a few hours, several scenic towns along the way and several trains a day make this route a good one to stop off and explore over

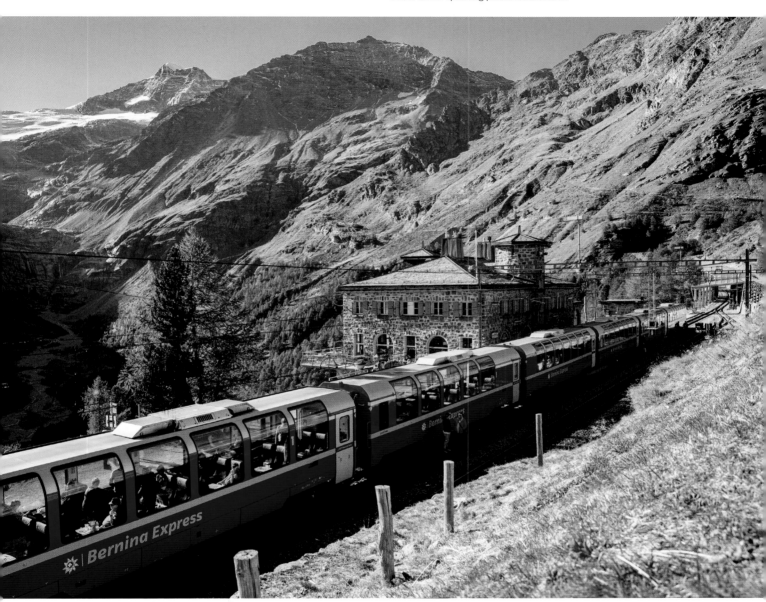

Passengers can alight at Alp Grüm to admire the elevated views of the Bernina Railway that snakes down and around tight curves and spiral tunnels in the Italian-speaking part of Switzerland.

several days if time permits. Sections of the route are also included in the *Glacier Express* (page 84), and parts of the *Bernina Express* can be combined with this train.

While the *Glacier Express* and the *Bernina Express* tourist trains operate on sections of the Rhaetian Railway, the line is also very much the lifeblood for many locals, who regularly travel on the trains.

TRACK NOTES

The *Bernina Express* takes in superb high-mountain scenery, with the narrow-gauge railway climbing over the Bernina Pass to an altitude of 2,250 m (7,382 ft) above sea level. The pass is considered to be one of Europe's highest train crossings. The route passes through 84 tunnels and across 383 bridges on its scenic, mountainous journey. Brusio Viaduct is a famous nine-arched circular

Above Seat reservations on the *Bernina Express* are compulsory for special panorama trains.

Opposite Trains on this route pass through picturesque scenery of lakes, forests and steep mountains slopes like those around Lake Poschiavo.

spiral viaduct around which the train coils in order to negotiate a steep section of track.

On 29 October 2022, the Rhaetian Railway (RhB) claimed a Guinness World Record after the 1,906 m (6,253 ft) train passed along a section of 2.5 km (1.6 miles) of the narrow-gauge line from the Albula Tunnel in Preda to the Landwasser Viaduct near Filisur. The feat was achieved in late 2022, during the 175th anniversary of Switzerland's first railway, and involved 25 four-car electric Capricorn units. The trains crossed 48 bridges and passed through 22 tunnels on the one-hour journey.

WELCOME ABOARD

The train officially starts at its eastern end in Tirano, Italy, but the *Bernina Express* Bus from Lugano in Ticino, Switzerland, connects to Tirano and passes beautiful alpine scenery on the way, including vineyards and Lake Como. Direct regional trains operated by Trenord from Milan connect through to Tirano.

Trains depart Tirano and start climbing without cogwheel traction towards the highest point on the route, Alp Grüm at 2,091 m (6,860 ft). The line passes through Brusio and enthusiasts may want to alight here to walk to the base of the famous circular viaduct to photograph the next passing train.

The line continues past the alpine Lake Poschiavo (Lago di Poschiavo), gripping its western shore close to the main road, and passing Le Presse, a small town with several boutique hotels and an abundance of recreational activities to make it a suitable stop for those who want to break the journey.

The next main town is Poschiavo, located in the Poschiavo Valley (Val Poschiavo) on the railway and road connecting Italy via the Bernina Pass. Its cobblestone streets and piazzas are Italian inspired, as are its local dishes and wines, which provide good reasons to alight here from the train. Not surprisingly, most residents speak Italian, and its courtly nineteenth-century architecture is Renaissance in style.

Another stop to consider alighting at is Alp Grüm, to admire the track that snakes down and around tight curves and spiral tunnels back to Cavaglia, from where the train has just ascended. It is clearly visible from Alp Grüm, some 400 m (1,300 ft) back down the line below. The current station building, together with its buffet and hotel, was opened in 1923, and its veranda is the ideal place to admire the next train climbing up the spirals. At Alp Grüm,

the train departs Graubünden (or Grisons) and the Romansh-speaking part of Switzerland (French, German and Italian are the three other official languages in Switzerland).

The line continues to pass the foreshore of the picturesque Lake Bianco (Lago Bianco) on its run down to Pontresina in the Bernina Valley (Val Bernina) that branches off the Upper Engadin Valley. Pontresina is a tourist destination with hotels and good infrastructure, but is overshadowed by its glitzy neighbour, St Moritz. Located in the Engadin Valley, St Moritz, at an altitude of 1,775 m (5,823 ft), hosted the Winter Olympics in 1928 and 1948, and continues to attract skiers who make the most of the ski runs and the plethora of après-ski activities.

Samedan in the Upper Engadin Valley is a twelfth-century village with a central square and a 400-year-old Reformed Church.

Albula Tunnel, with a maximum elevation of 1,820 m (5,970 ft), is one of the highest tunnels in the Alps. The 5,865 m (19,242 ft) tunnel opened in 1903 to connect the Albula Valley with the Engadin Valley. A second tunnel has been built to enable more trains to use the line.

Passengers can alight at Filisur for the line to Davos. Just beyond, at Teifencastel, the Church of St Stefan is a dominant feature on the left-hand side of the track. It is listed as a Swiss heritage site of national significance, with the original church dating back to the mid-fourteenth century.

Chur, Switzerland's oldest town, is also a rail junction for the train to Arosa and mainline trains from Zurich to Brig. It is the capital of Graubünden Canton and a city of historic significance, having been a site of civilized habitation for nearly 5,000 years. Rhätische Bahn (RhB) has a yard here, as well as being the beginning of the branch line to Arosa. This is an interesting line as it runs through the streets of Chur on its way out of town and up the mountain.

Passengers can change at Chur to an SBB train or continue on RhB's line northwards to Landquart on a line that runs parallel to SBB's standard-gauge tracks. The RhB track continues from Landquart up to Klosters, where the lines diverge again. One line goes to Davos and continues southwards to Filisur (on the Albula route), while the other is the Vereina Line. The latter includes the world's longest narrow-gauge railway mountain tunnel, of 19 km (12 miles). This line to Sagliains and Scuol opened in 1999.

ATTENTION TO DETAIL

While it is possible to travel the route within a day, regular trains along the route make it possible to alight at key destinations, then join a subsequent train. Passengers can upgrade to panoramic cars to better admire the journey. Swiss Travel Passes are valid on the entire *Bernina Express* journey, and seat reservations are compulsory for the panorama trains and the bus from Lugano to Tirano.

Both first- and second-class travel is available on panoramic and regional trains.

Bernina panoramic cars are used in the autumn and winter in combination with regular regional trains that operate hourly. The *Bernina Express* Bus to Tirano does not operate in winter. These cars are placed on several trains each day and are available for a slight surcharge on regular fares and for those travelling with a pass. They have panoramic windows, more spacious seating, refreshments and on-board commentary. Regional trains provide the same great views, and stop at every station for those who want to break their journey. Alpine Classic Pullman trains occasionally travel on this line.

Opposite The train negotiates several tight turns on the journey.

Right Numerous stone viaducts over wild alpine stream are a feature of the *Bernina Express*.

Below This panoramic train passes through the UNESCO World Heritage Site of the Rhaetian Railway.

GLACIER EXPRESS

SLOWEST EXPRESS TRAIN

Since 1930, the *Glacier Express* has travelled one of the world's most beautiful rail routes. This famous scenic train operates between the glamorous alpine resort towns of St Moritz and Zermatt. The journey of 291 km (181 miles) takes some eight hours, making it one of the world's slowest express trains, moving at a maximum speed of 90 km/h (56 mph) and an average speed of just 36 km/h (22 mph). Few passengers complain, as they are travelling in sleek, modern carriages with expansive panoramic windows while admiring Switzerland's stunning alpine and riverine landscapes. Glaciers are not a dominant feature of the landscape beside the track but are located higher up in the mountains. St Moritz and Zermatt provide very different experiences, depending on the season.

TRACK NOTES

Glacier Express trains are operated by the Matterhorn Gotthard Bahn (MGB) and Rhätische Bahn (RhB), with 140 km (87 miles) on the former and 151 km (94 miles) on the latter. The train negotiates 91 tunnels and crosses 291 bridges and viaducts, with the most famous being the Landwasser Viaduct at a height of 65 m (213 ft).

The *Glacier Express* operates on a section of MGB narrow gauge (1,000 mm, 3 ft 3⅜ in) track from Disentis in Graubünden to Zermatt in the Valais. The MGB network is an adhesion railway that uses Abt rack assistance on the steeper inclines, extending over 29 km (18 miles).

The line formerly crossed the Furka Pass between Realp and Oberwald at an elevation of 2,162 m (7,093 ft), with a 2 km (1.2 mile) tunnel passing beneath the pass. This compares to an elevation of 1,564 m (5,131 ft) in the current Furka Base Tunnel, which is 15 km (9.5 miles) long. The old scenic line, which is very attractive to tourists, is operated by the Dampfbahn Furka-Bergstrecke (DFB or Furka Heritage Railway) using heritage steam engines.

WELCOME ABOARD

The big decisions travellers have to make are what class (first, second or excellence on some services) and package they will choose, and in which direction they will take the train. However, an overnight stay in St Moritz and Zermatt is highly recommended before and after the all-day train journey. The other possibility is to join the train along the route, although the full journey is highly recommended. Trains depart on most mornings from both ends of the route, and passengers can join or leave the train at various stops along the way, with the main stations being Filisur (for Davos), Chur, Disentis, Andermatt and Brig. Independent travellers can take the same route by using various regional trains that work sections of the track.

Arrive in St Moritz via the *Bernina Express* for the morning departure of the *Glacier Express*, which departs every day except from mid-October to mid-December. Passengers can also board at Filisur via a connecting regional train from Davos.

The train proceeds via Tiefencastel, the Landwasser Viaduct, and down to Chur, a major junction for the main train line between Zurich and Brig along parts of the Rhine Valley. At an altitude of 585 m (1,919 ft), Chur is the lowest point along the route and is also where some passengers choose to join the train.

The route follows the River Rhine beyond Chur, then a tributary on its way to Disentis for a change of locomotive. The cogwheel on this loco is engaged in parts to assist the train in negotiating the steep sections along the track. Just before Andermatt, the train ascends the Oberalp Pass at 2,033 m (6,670 ft), passing through a series of ladder-like horseshoe curves.

The *Glacier Express* crosses the famous single-track Landwasser Viaduct.

Andermatt Station, located in the saddle of the historic Gotthard Pass, is much higher than, but nearly directly above, the SBB standard-gauge Gotthard Tunnel. Andermatt is a strategically located alpine village on the old north–south trade route across the Alps, whose main street is lined with wooden heritage buildings. A branch line from Andermatt to the SBB station at Göschenen is an exciting 4 km (2.5 miles) narrow-gauge one that ascends a very steep 18 per cent grade. It is a dramatic climb through snow sheds and tunnels, making for a short but memorable and scenic journey.

Above Fiesch, forests give way to a more barren alpine landscape, which is best appreciated in midwinter when thick snow blankets the ground. This portion of the line was largely completed in 1926. However, the original 2,162 m (7,093 ft) crossing of the Furka Pass was only opened in warmer seasons, while in the winter the tracks were lifted across avalanche zones. When the new Furka Base Tunnel opened, this older route ceased to function as the main line.

The line declines sharply through the Rhône River Valley just before Brig. The highlight of railway engineering is the 270-degree loop through which the train spirals down into the valley. At Brig, MGB's narrow-gauge line stops to enable an easy transfer to standard-gauge mainline trains, making this a popular transfer station for trains to other parts of Europe, including Domodossola (page 96).

To the north of Visp, the route of the Bern-Lötschberg-Simplon's old line climbs on a shelf towards the old Lötschberg Tunnel. At Visp, the train heads off the main line and begins climbing up from the valley on its journey southwards to Zermatt.

Passengers can alight at Brig, take a regional train to Visp and travel on the Post Bus to Visperterminen to sample the famous white wine made here from Heida grapes. The Valais (or Wallis) is Switzerland's largest wine-producing region, with its vineyards being some of Europe's highest. Chasselas or Fendant is grown in other parts of the canton, and the famous Raclette cheese is also produced here. Wines from the Valais are served on the train.

The *Glacier Express* terminates at its western end at Zermatt, high in the Alps. Car-free Zermatt is a popular year-round alpine holiday village where skiing and other snow sports dominate in the winter, while hiking is popular in the summer. The Matterhorn, at 4,478 m (14,692 ft), is one of the world's most recognizable landforms and the inspiration for the distinctive Toblerone chocolate. Its main street appeals to tourists for shopping, dining or après-ski relaxation over a locally brewed Zermatt Matterhorn beer in one of many bars. Visitors can dine on dishes such as *Älpermagrone* (alpine macaroni), cheese and cold cuts (more than 450 cheeses are made in Switzerland), fondue and air-dried beef.

In other parts of Switzerland, themed train journeys enable passengers to sample the two renowned Swiss dining delights of chocolate and cheese. These journeys include alighting from trains to admire where both are made or visiting museums that celebrate both delights.

ATTENTION TO DETAIL

New first- and second-class cars have elegant interiors and extensive panoramic windows to enable passengers to look up as well as out. Second- and first-class seats are configured as four seats with a centre aisle. Excellence Class has one seat on either side of the aisle (everyone gets a window seat, and there is a maximum of 20 passengers per carriage). Passengers in this class are served a six-course gourmet lunch, with wines paired with each course, plus afternoon tea.

Opposite The cogwheel Gornergrat Railway operates as a branch line beyond the Zermatt terminus of the *Glacier Express*. It travels up from the alpine resort village to near the base of the Matterhorn to offer commanding views of the majestic mountain and the surrounding alpine landscape.

Below In winter, sections of the *Glacier Express* route pass through snow so deep that the track seems to disappear. Snow-clearing equipment is often used in order to keep the line open before the express trains pass through.

Carriages on the *Glacier Express* are air cushioned for a quieter and smoother ride. Train facilities and services include on-board catering with freshly prepared meals, air conditioning, power points and a panoramic car with a bar. Detailed in-seat commentary is provided via headphones in six languages (English, French, German, Italian, Japanese and Chinese). There are facilities, including toilets, for wheelchair passengers in first-class carriages.

While those holding Eurail Passes have access to the *Glacier Express*, seat and/or seat reservations are compulsory and chargeable. Occasional nostalgic journeys are made on the Alpine Classic Pullman Express, hauled by a Ge 6.6 crocodile locomotive.

GORNERGRAT RAILWAY

Passengers can stay overnight in Zermatt, then spend the next day taking in Europe's highest cogwheel and fully electrified railway to the summit of Gornergrat (3,089 m/10,135 ft) for dramatic views of the Matterhorn (4,478 m/14,690 ft).

The incorporation of cogwheel technology enables the train to ascend the incline grade of up to 20 per cent, almost twice as steep as MGB's main line. The departure point is just beyond the main train station in the middle of the village, and there are many departures every day of the year for the 33-minute journey of 9.4 km (5.8 miles). The vertical rise is 1,469 m (1,539 ft). On a clear day, it is possible to view 29 peaks that top 4,000 m (13,123 ft).

Europe's highest-altitude hotel, the 3100 Hotelkulm Gornergrat, is located at the summit and features a restaurant, an astronomical observatory and shops, as well as a sun terrace and chapel. Skiers have direct access to the slopes from here.

INTERLAKEN TO THE ALPS

RAILWAY TO THE ROOF OF EUROPE

Interlaken, the town in the Bernese Oberland between the two lakes of Brienz (Brienzersee) and Thun (Thunersee), is one of Switzerland's busiest holiday destinations in both summer and winter. It is also where many exhilarating railway journeys commence. There are two main stations here, with Interlaken West being close to Lake Thun and the main station of Interlaken East (Interlaken Ost) being closer to Lake Brienz. It is important to distinguish between the two as they are a kilometre apart. Interlaken West best serves trains heading towards Thun and on to Bern, while Interlaken East is the main station serving the mountain routes given below.

The famous alpine peaks of the Eiger, Mönch and Jungfrau rise in the south and can be viewed from the grassy Höhematte in front of the Victoria Hotel in the centre of Interlaken. Harder Kulm rises behind the town as a solid backdrop, with the funicular cable car to its summit providing excellent views of the Alps and the two lakes.

The main routes into the Swiss Alps are managed by Jungfraubahn Holding AG, and tickets are covered by a Swiss

Travel Pass or a Jungfrau Pass. Travelling to Jungfraujoch (the saddle between the Jungfrau and Mönch peaks) is the rail journey most visitors want to make because it places them in an amazing snow-covered setting at Europe's highest railway station and the world's ninth highest, Jungfraujoch at 3,454 m (11,332). As a point of reference, Tangula Station on the Tibetan Plateau, at an altitude of 5,068 m (16,627 ft), is the world's highest railway station.

TRACK NOTES

The line to Jungfraujoch, conceived by Swiss industrial magnate and entrepreneur Adolf Guyer-Zeller, opened in 1912. Alpine tourism had already blossomed in Switzerland as adventurous and affluent tourists from across Europe travelled there to conquer the mountainous peaks, and patients stricken with tuberculosis came to recuperate in the clear mountain air.

The biggest challenge for Guyer-Zeller and his 100-strong team of mostly Italian labourers was to carve a tunnel through the Alps to Jungfraujoch, just below the summits of the Eiger and Mönch Mountains. The work was challenging, hard and dangerous due to rock falls, avalanches and dynamite-blasting accidents. Work began in 1896, and 16 years later the first train travelled from Kleine Scheidegg along the route of 9.3 km (5.8 miles) to the Jungfraujoch.

The dangerous work resulted in 30 deaths and 90 injuries. Guyer-Zeller died from pneumonia during the railway's construction, but family members continued work on the tunnel. However, progress was slow and the project faced financial difficulties, and in 1905 work was suspended once Eismeer Station had opened. Work then recommenced, and by 1912 the tunnel to the summit was finally completed.

Now, various trains are used on the railways into Interlaken and beyond to the mountains. Ten modern, low-floor panorama trains, each with a seating capacity of 152, entered service on the Grindelwald-Kleine Scheidegg route in 2005 and on the Lauterbrunnen-Kleine Scheidegg route in 2014.

WELCOME ABOARD

Interlaken is where several railway journeys into the Alps depart. The town began as a tourist centre and remains one of Switzerland's

Left A Swiss train passing the Thun Sea (Thunersee) during winter on its way to Interlaken.

Below left A train of the Jungfrau Railway waiting to depart from Kleine Scheidegg Railway Station to its Jungfraujoch terminus.

most vibrant travel destinations. Well-to-do German and English tourists identified Interlaken as a base for adventures in nature in the mid-nineteenth century. Grand hotels such as the Victoria-Jungfrau Grand Hotel and Spa and the Lindner Grand Hotel Beau-Rivage were built to cater to affluent visitors, and they continue to provide impeccable service. Victorian-era poets, artists and writers helped put the region on the map.

A smorgasbord of global cuisines provided in the town's restaurants reflects the ever-changing tourism demographics in a town that now attracts visitors in all seasons from around the

globe. While the producers of various James Bond films have a soft spot for Switzerland, it is more likely to be a Bollywood movie being filmed on location in the Swiss Alps these days. Popular K-drama *Crash Landing on You* incorporated locations around Interlaken in its filming. This is not lost on Switzerland Tourism, which recognizes that with each film come new waves of tourists eager to take selfies in the setting where the action unfolded.

LAUTERBRUNNEN TO MÜRREN

One of the more interesting railway journeys in this part of Switzerland is on the railway line from above the Lauterbrunnen Valley to Mürren. Passengers need to depart from Interlaken East and alight at Lauterbrunnen. It is only a 20-minute journey, with departures at least every 30 minutes, mostly during daylight hours.

The valley in which Lauterbrunnen is located is fascinating, since it contains some 72 waterfalls cascading down the steep slopes. At the end of the main street, Staubbach Waterfall is Europe's highest free-falling waterfall, while Trümmelbachfälle is further up the valley and accessible via the Post Bus, which departs Lauterbrunnen Station and heads up the valley to the Stechelberg cable car. From here, the cable car proceeds up the escarpment to the southern end of Mürren. Nineteenth-century English poet Lord Byron was so taken by the alpine setting with its glaciers and waterfalls, that he described Staubbach Falls as 'the tail of a white horse streaming in the wind'. He and other writers of the era did what modern-day 'influencers' continue to do by promoting tourism in the area.

It is just a short walk from Lauterbrunnen Station to the cable-car station, which travels up the escarpment to Grütschalp. Bearing in mind that Mürren is car free, visitors must decide whether to take this route or the Stechelberg cable car. Both are recommended and the final decision for those staying overnight may be which one provides the easiest access to their hotel.

Train enthusiasts will choose the narrow-gauge train mountain railway to Mürren (Bergbahn Lauterbrunnen-Mürren), which departs from Grütschalp. At 4.3 km (2.7 miles) in length, this railway is the shortest railway in the region and yet one of the most scenic.

The best views of the Alps and the Lauterbrunnen Valley are on the left-hand side of the two-car unit as it heads up the gentle incline to Mürren. While travelling on the train, passengers may want to contemplate exactly what these railcars are actually doing in such an elevated position and how they were positioned on the plateau 850 m (2,789 ft) above Lauterbrunnen. Before the cable car, there was a cogwheel railway from Lauterbrunnen to Grütschalp, and all the rolling stock was hauled up on this steep railway.

The railway opened in 1891 on a 1 m (3 ft 3 in) gauge track. Now electrified, it operates at just 30 km/h (18.6 mph). In 1967, two electric motor units (EMUs) were introduced and they remain in operation. However, the CFe 2/4 No. 11 motorcar, dating back to 1913, is maintained for nostalgic trips. Winteregg is the only stop along the way, and the restaurant here provides magical views of the region's three main peaks.

The cable car and train ride take just 20 minutes to reach Mürren from Lauterbrunnen, with services operating every 30 minutes from 6.30 a.m. to 5 p.m. Mürren is a pedestrian-only alpine town situated at an altitude of 1,650 m (5,413 ft). The station is located on the northern edge of the village, and it is a 1 km (3,280 ft) easterly walk through the settlement to the Gimmelwald cable-car station, which provides an alternate descent back to Stechelberg and on to Lauterbrunnen.

Energetic visitors may want to retrace their steps in walking from Mürren back to Grütschalp for the journey back down to Lauterbrunnen. This forested downhill walk provides excellent views of the Alps and of the trains passing along the line. It can also be done in reverse (Grütschalp to Mürren), but this option is uphill and more demanding than the downhill traverse.

One of the big attractions of Mürren is riding the cable car to the summit of Schilthorn (2,970 m/9,744 ft), where the classic 1968 James Bond film, *On Her Majesty's Secret Service*, starring Australian George Lazenby, was filmed (Switzerland has also featured in other Bond films, including *Goldfinger* and *Goldeneye*). There is a display about the film in the upper cable-car terminus and informative signs ('Walk of Fame') outside. Additionally, a Bond-themed buffet and 007 martinis, shaken not stirred, are available for diehard James Bond fans.

Mürren appeals as a year-round destination for many reasons. Heading the list are its remoteness and the fact that there is no road access from the outside world. Other endearing qualities are that it has a village atmosphere, numerous boutique hotels, inviting restaurants and simply stunning views of the Eiger, Mönch and Jungfrau Mountains.

Opposite A train of the Jungfrau Railway descending from the Jungfrau beyond Eiger Glacier Station (Eigergletscher).

LAUTERBRUNNEN–WENGEN–KLEINE SCHEIDEGG–JUNGFRAU

Trains operated by the Bernese Oberland Railway (Berner Oberland-Bahn) depart from Interlaken East Station for the journey to Lauterbrunnen, then on to Kleine Scheidegg for Jungfraujoch. As a rule, two train compositions operate to Zweilütschinen, where they are separated. One train continues to Lauterbrunnen and the other to Grindelwald. The right-hand side of the train provides marginally better views.

Trains between Lauterbrunnen, Wengen, Kleine Scheidegg and Grindelwald are operated in the distinctive green and yellow livery of the Wengernalp Railway. Passengers arriving from Interlaken change trains here, and if the train is crowded it is best to do this quickly to be assured of a seat. Again, the best views when ascending the mountain are on the right, looking down on the Lauterbrunnen Valley with its Staubbach Waterfall, and up to the Jungfrau and its neighbouring snow-capped peaks. The train ascends slowly from Lauterbrunnen to Kleine Scheidegg at 2,061 m (6,762 ft) above sea level, and serves as a feeder train to the Jungfrau Railway. Covering 19 km (12 miles), the route is the world's longest continuous rack railway. The busiest section of the track is between Lauterbrunnen and Wengen.

The journey from Lauterbrunnen to Wengen takes 12 minutes, while it is another 16 minutes to Kleine Scheidegg, making a total journey time of 38 minutes. Kleine Scheidegg has a lodge, restaurants and bars as it is a popular skiing field.

From Kleine Scheidegg, a change of train is required for Jungfraujoch, and although the journey is mostly through a tunnel, the left-hand side provides the best views as there are vistas through the Eiger North Face down the valley. Stops along the way include Eigerwand, a huge opening carved through the rock enabling those on the train to admire the view.

This 50-minute ride to its highest station, the Jungfraujoch, is on Europe's longest rack railway. Another stop is Eigergletscher, where the Eiger Express cable cars from Grindelwald offer other possibilities to the train. The train also stops at Eismeer Station before pulling into what is known as, the 'roof of Europe'.

Europe's highest railway station sits beneath a glacial saddle between the Jungfrau and Mönch peaks. From the underground station, visitors reach the surface via an elevator that provides access to the visitors' centre, restaurants, shops and facilities. Visitors can view Switzerland's largest glacier, the Aletsch, from an outdoor terrace located at the Sphinx Observatory, situated at an altitude of 3,571 m (11,716 ft). A research station for astronomical studies and other scientific pursuits has operated here since 1931. The station is one of the foremost environmental research stations for meteorology, glaciology, climate change and atmospheric measurements.

Facilities beneath the Jungfrau summit are extensive, and a terrace provides uninterrupted views of the Aletsch Glacier (recognized as the Swiss Alps Jungfrau-Aletsch UNESCO World Heritage Site), Switzerland's largest. Visitors can walk through the Ice Palace that has been carved through the surrounding glacier.

There are numerous outdoor activities, too, including sledding, tubing, skiing, snowboarding, zip-lining and glacial walks. Most visitors are happy to just take in the scenery, then return to the indoor warmth of the dining facilities. There are numerous dine-in or takeaway dining and bar facilities at Jungfraujoch. Lindt Chocolate Heaven provides a window on Swiss chocolate making, plus retail outlet shopping, while other shops sell souvenirs.

On the return journey down the mountain, passengers seeking exercise in the fresh air and the possibility of photographing trains going up and down the Jungfrau line can alight at Eigergletscher and walk down the well-formed trail to Kleine Scheidegg. Naturally, it is possible to do this in reverse, but being uphill this is more demanding. The downhill walk takes just one hour but could be longer depending on the activities conducted.

On arriving in Kleine Scheidegg, visitors change trains for either Grindelwald or Wengen for their homeward journey to Interlaken. Completing the loop via Grindelwald is recommended. This looped journey can be done in reverse, starting in Interlaken and travelling via Zweilütschinen, Grindelwald, Kleine Scheidegg, Jungfraujoch, Wengen and Lauterbrunnen, before returning to Interlaken in the late afternoon.

KLEINE SCHEIDEGG–GRINDELWALD–INTERLAKEN EAST

The descent from Kleine Scheidegg via Grindelwald/Grund takes 24 minutes. Passengers travelling in organised groups may have to alight at Grund, where coaches are normally parked as there is only limited space for them in Grindelwald. The remaining passengers disembark soon after at Grindelwald for their train back to Interlaken East following the glacier-fed Schwarze Lütschine River.

Grindelwald is a wonderful alpine village with good tourism infrastructure. The railway station is in the middle of town, and is where trains operated by the Bernese Oberland Railway depart for Interlaken and where trains on the Wengernalp Railway arrive from Kleine Scheidegg. Trains from Grindelwald depart approximately every 30 minutes and take 35 minutes to reach Interlaken East.

Visitors may consider taking the gondola to First for activities such as the First Flyer, Cliff Walk, skiing, hiking, and riding a Trotti bike downhill to Grindelwald.

INTERLAKEN EAST TO SCHYNIGE PLATTE

This mountainous location is accessible via the Schynige Platte Railway, which operates from Wilderswil with connections to Interlaken. Schynige Platte is a small mountain ridge providing splendid views of the Alps and lakes from its terminus station, located at an altitude of 1,967 m (6,453 ft). This mountain cogwheel railway opened in 1893 and remains one of the highest in Switzerland. While electrified traction replaced steam locomotives a long time ago, the heritage train dates back over a century, and the wooden carriage seats are original. It takes the train 52 minutes to cover the vertical climb of 7 km (4.3 miles) to the summit.

Berghotel Schynige Platte is a short walk from the station, and its rooms and Panorama Restaurant on the terrace have commanding alpine views. Packages that include rail transfers, accommodation, dinner and breakfast offer the best value for those who want to stay the night.

The Schynige Platte Alpine Botanical Garden is accessible via a well signposted trail that provides a valuable insight into more than 600 species of alpine vegetation. Other trails head off from

here, including destinations such as Loucherhorn, Faulhorn and First, with the latter providing access to Grindelwald via an aerial gondola.

Above The cogwheel railway to Schynige Platte passes through rolling alpine meadows close to Breitlauenen, the small mid-station stop.

Opposite The cogwheel railway from Wilderswil to Schynige Platte only operates from early June to late October.

ATTENTION TO DETAIL

Many of these trains operate every day of the year, especially those in the valley sectors. Sections of the mountain railways are closed for a few days for maintenance, but this is generally done later in the year when passenger numbers are lower. Trains operate at different hours, with those of the Jungfraubahn being from 9 a.m. to 6 p.m. daily with a mid-day break.

Swiss Travel Pass and Eurail Pass holders receive discounts on the rail line to the Jungfrau and most other Swiss mountain railways. Family tickets and discounted children's tickets are also available (children under six years of age travel for free). Bookings are best made online.

Visitors to high altitudes need to be conscious of altitude sickness and cold weather. Descending to a lower altitude is the best way to alleviate altitude sickness.

With so many trains in and around Interlaken, choosing which journey to make is difficult. While the route to Jungfraujoch is essential for rail enthusiasts, it certainly is popular and crowded during peak times, which seem to be almost every day. While the trains to Mürren and Schynige Platte are short, they are appealing because they are less travelled and more hidden railway gems for those who like to travel to more remote destinations.

Mürren has additional appeal as it cannot be reached by public road. However, it is very popular year-round, although many tourists just visit for the day and stay elsewhere, ensuring that the evenings are less crowded. While Mürren has a permanent population of less than 500, there are 2,000 hotel beds, mostly in small establishments. One of the big attractions is that the village offers views of the three towering mountains: Jungfrau, Eiger and Mönch.

LOCARNO TO BRIG VIA DOMODOSSOLA

A JOURNEY THROUGH A HUNDRED VALLEYS

Almost any Swiss railway promises jaw-dropping scenery of alpine lakes, snow-capped mountains, rivers and lush pastures. The two-hour journey from Locarno (Switzerland) to Domodossola (Piedmont, Italy) on the Centovalli Railway is one of Europe's most picturesque. The railway is known as Centovallina in Switzerland and Vigezzina in Italy. The route traversing 100 valleys is operated by the Centovalli Express. The line opened in late 1923 with 30 stations, and extends for 52 km (32 miles) through valleys in which glacial-fed streams flow, waterfalls cascade down forested mountains, and remote villages and vineyards dot the landscape.

In his celebrated book *The Great Railway Bazaar by Train through Asia*, author Paul Theroux headed off on his 1974 Asian odyssey on the train through Domodossola. His cabin companion, Richard Cuthbert Duffill, from Barrow-upon-Humber in Lincolnshire, alighted at Domodossola Station to stretch his legs. The tale of the mysterious Duffill missing the train and Theroux's efforts to reunite him with his luggage in Venice, a few stops down the line, are a good read for dedicated train travellers.

The train to Domodossola also attracted author Bill Bryson, who described the journey as 'a spectacular ride along the lips of deep gorges and forbidding passes, where farmhouses and hamlets were tucked away in the most inaccessible places, on the edge of giddy eminences'.

TRACK NOTES

The route is operated by the Ferrovie Autolinee Regionali Ticinesi (FART) in Switzerland and the Società Subalpina Imprese Ferroviarie (SSIF) in Italy. Trains travel on mostly single, metre-gauge track with 32.3 km (20 miles) through Italy and 19.8 km (12.3 miles) in Switzerland. Two-car electric units are typical. Rail stock is being upgraded on the route with the introduction of panoramic trains, which may incur a supplement (*supplemento*) collected on the train by the conductor.

WELCOME ABOARD

The journey from Locarno to Domodossola begins in Ticino, the Italian-speaking Swiss canton. Switzerland's southernmost canton is located entirely south of the Alps and has a Mediterranean

ambiance. A side trip from Locarno to Bellinzona, the canton capital, before joining the train is recommended. Three castle fortresses in this railway junction town are on UNESCO's World Heritage List. The massive structures protected the medieval town, which is strategically located on a once-important trade route from Italy through Bellinzona to Germany. Bellinzona is on the main line from German-speaking Switzerland, through to Lugano, then southwards to Milan in Italy. Nearby, Lugano is also the departure point for the bus that travels across northern Italy to Tirano for the *Bernina Express* (page 78). Adjoining Ascona is Switzerland's lowest lying town at 196 m (643 ft). Its old town is lined with narrow streets with boutiques, restaurants and cafes.

Passengers can experience the sights and food of Ticino before joining the train. Like their Italian neighbours, the Ticinese live to eat. You can eat and drink in a *grotto* or village tavern, sampling Italian-inspired cuisine plus locally sourced wines and rice (Ticino is the world's northernmost rice-producing area). Specialities include minestrone soup, polenta with braised meat or roasted rabbit, salami, and cheeses like Piora or Zincarlin. Merlot wines (both red and white varieties), Grappa and Nocino (walnut-flavoured brandy) are produced in Ticino.

The journey begins in Locarno and generally heads westwards

Trains of the Centovalli Railway travel via Domodossola in Italy and connect the two Swiss towns of Locarno and Brig.

across a section of northern Italy to Domodossola. Locarno is located on the northern foreshore of picturesque Lake Maggiore near Ascona and just north of the Italian border. It is important to join the train at the appropriate platform – there are several platforms at Locarno Station. Occasionally, buses are used for the first section of the track when repairs are being made, or when the track is damaged. It is therefore important to inquire about this, especially if the platform is deserted when it should have at least a few passengers.

The line is ideal for those who want to alight at certain stations and rejoin the next train. Ponte Brolla, 10 minutes into the journey, is a good stop to alight at to explore and for walks into the Vallemaggia, through which the River Maggia flows. Farmers here also store cereal crops in wooden and stone buildings called *torba*.

Another possible stop for 360-degree views of the valley is the village of Intragna, just a short walk from the station. There is a tower from which the view can be admired, and just off the village piazza there is a museum. Highlights include the Isorno Bridge near the village of Intragna and Intragna's gorge.

Verdasio provides access to the cable car that ascends to the car-free village of Rasa. The Centovalli line continues through the rugged and mountainous Centovalli, and crosses the impressive steel deck-arch Ruinacci Viaduct built in 1915 to enter Camedo Station. Just beyond Camedo, the track enters Italy at Ribellasca and remains in Italy until it travels through the Simplon Tunnel.

Santa Maria Maggiore is the highest point of the railway at 831 m (2,726 ft). Visitors in winter can expect the small town to be dusted in snow, making for an atmospheric Advent market. The town has three museums: one celebrating local artists, another dedicated to perfume and – the most mysterious of all – one dedicated to chimney sweepers.

The medieval junction of Domodossola is the gateway to seven alpine valleys. The line northwards from Domodossola through the Simplon Tunnel and back into Switzerland resurfaces at Brig for connections to Visp and Chur. The journey to Domodossola takes about two hours, while Brig takes some three hours.

ATTENTION TO DETAIL

Trains from Basel, Bern and Milan pass through Ticino regularly, with one arriving every hour or so. Regional trains operated by

TILO also provide services within the canton. There are some 10 daily trains from Locarno to Domodossola, although there are also more frequent trains that only operate on a section of the track to Intragna and Camedo. The first train departs at 7.09 a.m., and the last one at 6.48 p.m.

Swiss Travel System offers overseas visitors a range of tickets that provide easy access to most bus, train and boat routes in the country. A Swiss Pass also enables travellers to visit more than 500 museums and receive discounts on many funiculars, cog railways and cable cars in Switzerland. Children under 16 years of age travelling with at least one pass-carrying adult travel for free. Passes are sold for durations of three, four, six, eight and 15 days. Flexible passes are also available. Luggage can be forwarded to a hotel via a station for a fee, enabling visitors to explore without having to lug their luggage. The Centovalli Railway is fully covered by Eurail and Swiss Travel Passes.

A connecting train from Lucerne to Bellinzona for Locarno was once known as the *Wilhelm Tell Express*. It has been renamed the *Gotthard Panorama Express*. This steam paddleboat and scenic train journey departs Lucerne (Luzern) and proceeds across the

Opposite The rail route through the 100 valleys passes some of Europe's most rugged and dramatic scenery.

Below Fewer passengers travel on the Centovalli Railway in winter, but those who do are rewarded with magical scenery.

lake on a Belle Epoque steam paddleboat. The route celebrates Swiss national hero Wilhelm Tell, who lived in Uri, which is passed on the boat journey. Passengers can have lunch on board the boat before it arrives in Flüelen. They join a first-class panoramic coach to make the journey to Lugano. Train lovers will appreciate the double-horseshoe curve at Wassen, where the mountainous village can be viewed from different angles as the railway passes through several helical spirals and tunnels to overcome the steep incline. It then passes through the Gotthard Tunnel, before emerging into Ticino with its Mediterranean ambiance and the appearance of Italian signs on all railway stations. The Gotthard Base Tunnel opened in 2016 after 17 years of construction to become the world's longest railway tunnel at 57 km (35 miles). While this new tunnel saves time, it misses the Wassen spirals. Passengers for Locarno and the train for Domodossola need to alight at Bellinzona for a local connection.

Visitors staying in Ticino hotels have access to the Ticino Ticket, which enables them and those sharing a room to enjoy complimentary second-class travel on all public transport in the canton. This can be arranged via a smartphone app or a printed ticket issued by accommodation providers. These passes are valid until midnight on the day of check out, and they also offer 20 per cent discounts on Swiss boat trips operating on the Swiss sections of Lakes Maggiore and Lugano.

GERMANY
RHINE RIVER LINE

COLOGNE TO MAINZ

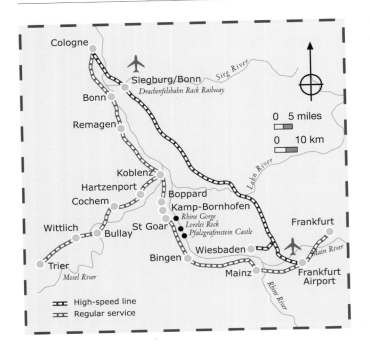

Map legend:
- High-speed line
- Regular service

German Railways, or Deutsche Bahn (DB), operate services along the heavily used and very scenic Middle Rhine (Mittelrhein). Historically, the River Rhine (or Rhein), 232 m (766 miles) long, is one of Europe's most significant rivers. It begins at Lake Toma in Graubünden Canton, high in the Swiss Alps, and flows through Liechtenstein, Austria, Germany, France and the Netherlands, to empty into the North Sea near the busy port of Rotterdam.

Having long served as a principal European trade route, much of the Rhine is still a major navigable waterway. It was only logical that the main railways would follow its course. The rail route from Basle, Switzerland, to Cologne (Köln), Germany, is among Europe's most important intercity lines. These lines experience not only a continual flow of local and intercity passenger trains, but also an increasing number of freight trains. Changes brought about by the European Union have opened up continental railways, and the strategic lines through the Rhineland are appealing to freight operators. Where DB was once the sole operator, the lines are now shared by a variety of companies, including freight trains run by SBB (Swiss Federal Railways).

Since the opening of the 177 km (110 mile), Cologne to Frankfurt high-speed line in 2002, fast and frequent ICE (Intercity Express Services) have been departing at regular intervals along this new line, instead of using the slower lines on either side of the Rhine. While the high-speed route is an hour faster, it misses the scenic vineyards, hilltop fortresses and historic villages that can be seen along the older lines.

The scenic routes from Cologne to Mainz (152 km/94 miles) and the detour up the Mosel Valley are the most picturesque in the Middle Rhine.

TRACK NOTES

There are many ways to approach this rail journey, depending on the time available and the direction of travel. The route is made up of several railway lines that are roughly parallel on both sides of the Rhine. The route's scenic beauty is enhanced by the region's rich history of ancient fortifications, medieval castles, and numerous historical towns and cities with their old half-timber buildings. While a train journey from Cologne to Mainz takes two and a half hours, for some, several days or weeks would not be long enough to take in all that the route offers. Almost every train in the DB's inventory passes along the Rhine.

WELCOME ABOARD

Rail enthusiasts opt to travel along the Rhine's most scenic route, as the high-speed rail sacrifices scenery for expedience. International travellers can begin their journey at Frankfurt Airport on their arrival in Germany. The airport is connected by two railway stations, which make for an easy transfer from plane to train. Times of trains are displayed in the airport terminals, and train tickets can be bought to destinations across Europe.

A more traditional starting point is the Frankfurt Hauptbahnhof (Main Station), one of Germany's classic stations. Designed by Georg P. H. Eggert and completed in 1879, the station features a cavernous, triple-span iron shed that is 186 m (610 ft) long and was initially conceived to cover 18 tracks. Its design became a model for several other railway stations across Europe and America.

However, the journey proper along the Rhine starts at Mainz, which is accessible by regular services from both Frankfurt Airport and its Main Station. Heading northwards along the Rhine from Mainz, travellers have a choice of using the left-bank route or the right. For a complete experience, plan a round trip on one line and back on the other. Historically, express trains used the faster left-bank line, leaving the right-bank line for freight trains and all-stop local trains. However, freight and local trains frequent both lines, although express trains are less frequent than they once were. The continual passing of trains makes for a great train-watching experience on the journey down the river. The lighting conditions for photography are better when travelling northwards from Frankfurt along the right bank, then returning via the left.

The most scenic section of the journey is along the sinuous gorge north of Mainz between Bingen and Koblenz. It is recognized by UNESCO as a World Heritage Site for its dramatic scenery and historic architectural landmarks. Near Kaub (on the right bank), Pfalzgrafenstein, a famous castle, is situated on an island in the middle of the Rhine. It was built in the fourteenth century by the King of Germany and Holy Roman Emperor Ludwig IV

Opposite A class 101 electric locomotive hauling an intercity (IC) train through Andernach on the west bank of the Rhine River.

Below A T series 415 (double-unit) high-speed, intercity express (ICE) train operated by Deutsche Bahn near St Goarshausen.

to extort tolls from ships using the river. Today, this section is very popular with tourists who arrive from Kaub by ferry. The historic walled town of Oberwesel is nearby on the left bank, and the track runs adjacent to its ancient medieval towers. Schönburg Castle overlooks the town, and there are some excellent views of passing trains here.

The Mittelrhein has a few bridges, and small ferries shuttle cars and passengers across the river. One of these operates between St Goarshausen (on the left bank) and St Goar, a quaint town settled in the sixth century, located near the thirteenth-century Burg Rheinfels (a picturesque ruined castle best viewed from the left bank).

At Boppard (on the left bank), the river makes a sharp 'S'-bend, famous for its picturesque setting and difficult navigation. Here the left-bank railway travels inland, as hotels and restaurants line the town's 'Rheinallee' riverside promenade. Several hotels near the station make this an ideal town to stop at for the night. Historic baths dating back to the Roman occupation are located beneath the main Marktplatz.

The remainder of the journey towards Cologne is pleasant, although not as scenic as the earlier section. Bonn, Beethoven's birthplace and capital of the German Federal Republic during the Cold War, is an interesting stop. Not far from Bonn on the right bank, Königswinter is the location of the volcanic crag called Drachenfels (Dragon Rock). The aptly named Drachenfelsbahn Rack Railway takes visitors to the summit.

The Cologne Hauptbahnhof is an impressive station at which to begin or conclude this journey. This distinctive station was designed by J. E. Jacobsthal and represents an unusual European design, where the tracks are elevated above the street and the station is below the shed. Both the station and Cologne's monumental cathedral, whose tower looms 157 m (515 ft) above, were badly damaged during the Second World War, but both have been repaired.

The Mittelrhein's parallel left- and right-bank main lines connecting picturesque villages and towns, combined with scenic splendour, make this one of Europe's most picturesque rail journeys.

Opposite top An intercity express (ICE 3) class 406 train and a regional train at Cologne Central Station.

Opposite below A Deutsche Bahn cargo freight train, hauled by a class 185 electric locomotive, crossing South Bridge in Cologne.

ATTENTION TO DETAIL

Tickets can be bought online or at stations. Interrail passes are valid on this line and discounts are offered on KD Rhine Line boats. Regional Express trains connect Koblenz with Trier and most stations in between. Luxembourg National CFL trains run (four-car double-decker trains of the 2300 series, type KISS, manufactured by Stadler). Trains to Luxembourg via Trier operate at two-hour intervals throughout the day.

RIVER MOSEL DETOUR

A fascinating detour involves travelling part of the way up the River Mosel, one of the Rhine's main tributaries. This journey commences in Koblenz on the river's left bank, 79 km (49 miles) south of Cologne. From its headwaters high in France's Vosges Mountains, the Mosel (Moselle in French) flows through one of Europe's most beautiful valleys to Koblenz (corrupted from the Latin word meaning 'confluence'). This scenic railway runs through the Mosel Valley to the ancient city of Trier, which dates back 4,000 years.

Railway bridges north and south of Koblenz enable trains serving the right bank to access Koblenz Hauptbahnhof. This is ideal for passengers seeking to switch from one side of the river to the other. On the right bank, opposite the city, stands the impressive Ehrenbreitstein citadel fortress.

Not far from Koblenz Station, the railway crosses the Mosel and closely follows the left bank for the next 50 km (31 miles). The Mosel is Germany's most acclaimed wine region, with its steep, terraced vineyards situated on south-facing slopes to maximize their exposure to sunlight. Picturesque churches and castles like the ones at Kobern-Gondorf and Burg Eltz dot the valley.

Also popular with visitors is the village of Cochem, where ample accommodation and restaurants cater to tourists. Between the stations at Neef and Bullay the track grips the right bank of the Mosel, where vineyards flourish on the steep banks on both sides of the river. Bullay is an iconic Mosel village where the railway crosses the river on a long, double-deck truss bridge that carries vehicles on the lower level. Soon after, the line strays well away from the river and does not rejoin it until the Roman city of Trier, 185 km (115 miles) upriver from Koblenz. Wine lovers who want to visit famous villages such as Zeltingen-Rachtig and Bernkastel-Kues are able to catch buses that connect to the rail line.

HARZER SCHMALSPURBAHNEN

A STEAM-DOMINATED NETWORK

Trainspotters can head off from Germany's main rail network to explore the beauty of the narrow-gauge railway that serves the Harz Mountains, Germany's northernmost mountain range. The network, located between Hanover and Leipzig, consists of three railways: the Harzquerbahn, Selketalbahn and Brockenbahn. Known collectively as the HSB after all three railways, it operates daily services that are still mostly hauled by steam locomotives. The railway's inventory of 25 steam locomotives, 10 railcars, 12 diesel locomotives and 137 carriages is as impressive as the mountain scenery.

The railway was conceived in the 1880s, making it a relative latecomer to the era of rail travel in this part of Germany. The current network evolved from two separate systems that were mostly built in the 1880s and '90s and did not connect until 1905.

The Harz Mountains region was awkwardly situated on the post-war militarized border between East and West Germany, resulting in many areas being off-limits during the Cold War. Yet East Germany's constrained economic development paradoxically ensured the survival of this narrow-gauge railway as part of the national Deutsche Reichsbahn network. It was the most extensive of East Germany's seven surviving narrow-gauge railways, but due to the lack of investment it continued to operate steam locomotives decades after most lines in the West had been either electrified or converted to diesel locomotion. The German reunification in 1990 led to a consolidation of the German railway network. At that time, the Harz Mountain lines were trimmed from the national rail system and established as a private railway under the name Harzer Schmalspurbahnen GmbH. The continued operation of steam locomotives was viewed as a virtue that would attract tourists rather than face burdensome obsolescence. As a result, steam locomotives were not only retained but also maintained with regular daily departures throughout the year. Consequently, the network is a popular tourist attraction and one of the few places in the world still operating regular timetabled steam trains. Now, over one million passengers travel on the network, which operates 500,000 km (311,000 miles) of public and tourist trips per year.

TRACK NOTES

The metre-gauge Harzer Schmalspurbahnen is one of the world's last great steam adventures, with many steam locomotives in its inventory. Although popular with visitors, the network of 140 km (87 miles) is far more than a train for tourists, as it also functions as a key part of the region's transport network. The network is divided into three distinctive sections reflecting both the line's history and contemporary timetables. These services connect to various destinations, and cross-platform transfers allow for easy change of trains. Distances on the various lines are: Harzquerbahn (61 km / 38 miles), Selketalbahn (60 km / 37 miles) and Brockenbahn (19 km / 12 miles).

The steeply graded narrow-gauge railway requires specialized locomotives. The most common are 2-10-2T steam locomotives, which feature low driving wheels for great power at low speeds.

The majority of trains, including all trains to and from the Brocken, are hauled by steam locomotives, which are typically 2-10-2T tank engines built in the mid-1950s. These were the most powerful narrow-gauge steam locomotives ever built in Germany.

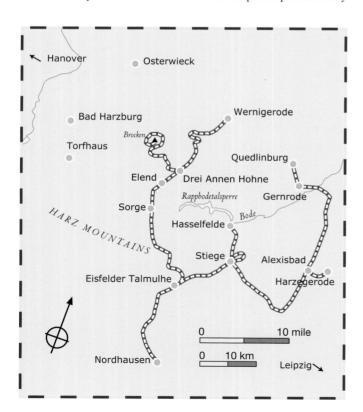

A steam-hauled train operated by the Harzer Schmalspurbahnen Brockenbahn crossing a stone bridge.

Some trains are powered by 1970s diesel locomotives, while diesel railcars are operated on local services. Rail enthusiasts should consult the railway's website to ensure they travel on the train they require.

Although as many as 10 steam locomotives may operate on the route each day, diesel-powered trains and self-propelled railcars augment the steam services. Historical steam-hauled trains, traversing scenery ranging from mountains to farmland over a decentralized network that connects numerous historic towns, ensure that this part of Germany is an essential destination for railway enthusiasts to visit. Pleasant surprises appear with almost every new station that these trains pass.

WELCOME ABOARD

Trains work the line every day between the UNESCO World Heritage town of Quedlinburg, the Thuringian town of Nordhausen, the colourful town of Wernigerode and Brocken Station. The latter is situated at the highest point along the route at an altitude of 1,125 m (3,691 ft).

The Harzquerbahn is the primary north–south line, running for 61 km (38 miles) to connect the industrial centre of Nordhausen with the popular medieval town of Wernigerode. Drei Annen Hohne (540 m/1,771 ft above sea level) is centred on the picturesque station located 46 km (29 miles) north of Nordhausen. The well-preserved station at Drei Annen Hohne is an operations centre for the railway. It is also the station where many passengers change trains for the famous Brockenbahn, which winds its way to the top of the Brocken. The Brockenbahn diverges from the Harzquerbahn just south of this station. This steeply graded line spirals its way up to the Brocken summit. In summer, this is the most intensively steam-operated portion of the railway. Immaculately maintained 2-10-2T locomotives proceed steadily up and down the slope. The 3.3 per cent climb (an increase in altitude of 1 m/ 3 ft 3 in for every 30 m/200 ft travelled) exacts a considerable strain on the locomotives. As such, steam locomotives must stop mid-journey at Schierke to take on more water for the boiler. The climb is accomplished at an exacting yet leisurely pace. As the line gains elevation, gaps in the trees hint at the vistas to be seen from

the summit. Visitors should bring warm clothing as blustery winds scour the mountaintop regardless of the season. During the Cold War, facilities at Brocken, including the railway station, housed soldiers who ran a Soviet listening post on the West. Several stark buildings are a legacy of the uninspired architecture that was so typical of the communist era. Facilities now include a history museum, botanical garden, weather station, restaurant and the Brocken Hotel. The hotel is the only accommodation available in the national park. It extends over eight floors with an observation deck and various dining options, including a cafe with a view on the seventh floor.

Visitors often neglect the third portion of the HSB network. The Selketalbahn joins the Harzquerbahn at Eisfelder Talmühle using the network's steepest grade. This route connects Eisfelder Talmühle with Gernrode and Quedlinburg, along with short branches to Hasselfelde and Harzgerode. Avoid the crowds and take the train through the forests on the Harzquerbahn from Wernigerode to Eisfelder Talmühle. Here, change trains on to the Selketal Railway to Quedlinburg.

Quedlinburg is a UNESCO World Heritage Site highly regarded for its outstanding Romanesque architecture, timber-framed buildings from at least five centuries, and medieval religious art displayed in the Church of St Servatius within the Quedlinburg Castle. It was an influential and prosperous trading centre during the early Middle Ages. Carl Ritter, one of the fathers of geography, was born in the small town. Quedlinburg is a very popular tourist destination because of its medieval architecture set amid a warren of cobblestone streets.

The scenery at this end of the network is more pastoral than the forests further west. Steam operations are focused on the Gernrode end of the Selketalbahn, while most through trains to Eisfelder Talmühle are diesel powered.

ATTENTION TO DETAIL

Trains to the Brocken operate a summer and winter timetable. Tickets can be bought online before departure, and seats can be reserved at least seven days in advance for a small surcharge. Tickets are sold one way to the Brocken or return, and discounts apply for groups of more than 20 passengers. Afternoon discounts and adult and child fares are offered (a child is considered as someone 6–14 years of age). Dog owners have to purchase a ticket for any pets in tow. Trains can be chartered for special events and large group excursions.

Many train passengers travel on the network to simply enjoy the ride and to take in the sights, while others are attracted to special train services such as the Advent Express (at Christmas), the Autumn Brunch Train, Murder Mystery Dinners, Santa Trains, Eastern Bunny Train, Gourmet Tours (while having a three-course lunch comprising local delicacies) and the Whisky Tasting Train.

Above Steam locomotive 99 6001-4 has operated on the Harzer Schmalspurbahnen Brockenbahn since the 1950s.

Opposite The metre-gauge railway operates all year round and is often referred to as 'the biggest among the little ones'.

Significantly, the narrow-gauge railway interfaces with the national railway network operated by Deutsche Bahn (DB) at Nordhausen, Quedlinburg and Wernigerode. In addition, a short portion of its line is shared with Nordhausen's tram network, making for an unusual but delightful rail experience in northern Germany.

ZUGSPITZBAHN

COGWHEEL TO THE TOP OF GERMANY

The narrow-gauge Bayerische Zugspitzbahn (Bavarian Zugspitze Railway) departs from the picturesque Bavarian town of Garmisch-Partenkirchen (often abbreviated to Garmisch-Partenk and nick-named 'Ga-Pa') in southern Germany. It travels along a line 19.5 km (12 miles) long to the summit of Zugspitze, Germany's highest mountain at 2,962 m (9,720 ft) above sea level. The line rises 883 m (2,897 ft) between the two terminus stations and is operated by the Bayerische Zugspitzbahn Bergbahn AG (BZB), whose majority owner is the Garmisch-Partenkirchen Municipal Works.

Work on the alpine railway began in 1928 and was completed in 1930 with a three-stage opening. The first sections to be opened in December 1929 were the 3.2 km (2 mile) centre section between Grainau and Eibsee and the 7.5 km (4.7 mile) track between Garmisch and Grainau. This provided access to a main line into Garmisch. The final section of 8.3 km (5.2 miles) from Eibsee to the summit station of Schneefernerhaus opened in mid-1930. This station, at 2,650 m (8,694 ft), is now closed to the general public, although research is conducted here by scientists. The final section features the Zugspitze Tunnel, 4.5 km (2.8 miles) in length.

In 1987, the summit route changed with the opening of the 975 m (3,199 ft) Rosi Tunnel. This new tunnel branches off about three-quarters of the way along the earlier tunnel. It operates through to the new and lower terminal of Zugspitzplatt, situated at 2,588 m (8,491 ft) above sea level.

The branch line to Zugspitzplatt extended the old line to its current distance of 19.5 km (12 miles). For five years, both stations were used, but the old route to Schneefernerhaus has not routinely operated since 1992.

The train does not go to the Zugspitze summit, but it is accessible via the Seilbahn Zugspitze from Eibsee or the Tyrolean Zugspitze Cable Car (to the south-west of Zugspitze in neighbouring Austria).

The route is especially popular in winter as it provides access to the alpine ski area known as Garmisch Classic. The area hosted the World Championships in 1978 and 2011, and alpine skiing debuted here at the 1936 Winter Olympics. The Garmisch Classic is known for the highly regarded Kandahar slope, which continues to host World Cup events in downhill, super G and giant slalom.

TRACK NOTES

The Zugspitzbahn is one of just a few German railways that still use a rack-and-pinion (cogwheel) system to negotiate the steep gradients along the route. This southern Bavarian railway is Germany's highest railway and one of the highest in Europe. The

route to the Zugspitze summit is on metre-gauge track that becomes a cogwheel line beyond Grainau.

For the first 7.5 km (4.7 miles) of the track, the train operates as an adhesion line to Grainau. The mountain section begins at Grainau with the 11.5 km (7.1 miles) of line equipped with a Riggenbach rack system developed and named by a Swiss engineer. The Vitznau-Rigi Railway in Switzerland incorporates his design.

WELCOME ABOARD

Visitors are recommended to arrive early for a relatively relaxed journey to the Zugspitze. Most visitors allocate at least three hours to participate in all the activities. The journey begins from the main station in the centre of this once-strategic market town at a height of 705 m (2,313 ft) above sea level. Here, the railway operates its own station, which is operationally entirely separate from the adjacent standard-gauge Deutsche Bahn (DB) station. It also retains the station name of Garmisch rather than Garmisch-Partenkirchen, which is used on the DB platforms. The two towns were contentiously amalgamated in 1935 by Adolf Hitler in preparation for the 1936 Winter Olympics.

The train stops at the main stations of Hausberg, Kreuzeck, Hammersbach, Grainau, Eibsee, Riffelriss, Gletscherbahnhof and

Above The rack rail was opened in sections between 1928 and 1930 to service holiday destinations such as lakeside Eibsee.

Opposite A train of the Zugspitzbahn on its way to its Garmisch-Partenkirchen terminus.

Zugspitzplatt, stopping at smaller stations only on request.

On leaving Garmisch-Partenkirchen, the electric train runs through the German countryside, past farmland, meadows and several small villages before it begins its climb. There is a stop at Hausberg for those who want to access the Hausbergbahn cable car. Kreuzeck is the stop for two other cable cars that rise up the slopes: the Kreuzeckbahn rises to Mount Kreuzeck at 1,651 m (5,420 ft), and the Alspitzbahn proceeds to Mount Osterfelderkopf at 2,057 m (6,749 ft). The first ski area at Kreuzeck was developed for the 1936 Winter Olympics in neighbouring Garmisch-Partenkirchen. Kreuzeck Valley Base Station served as the finishing line for the downhill section for part of the downhill skiing event. The Kreuzeckbahn, Germany's first mountain gondola, opened in 1926. The original Olympic course is still maintained and accessible.

The train stops in the small village of Hammersbach, where mountaineers and walkers may alight for the various outdoor

Right The Bavarian Zugspitze Railway is the highest railway in Germany and the third highest in Europe.

Opposite left The railway climbs steeply uphill from Grainau, travels past Eibsee Station and finally arrives at its terminus near the border with Austria.

Opposite right The lower half of the Zugspitzbahn operates in the open-air, while the upper half is underground.

adventures, climbing routes and alpine huts offered on the Wetterstein Mountains. The next stop is Grainau, with numerous boutique accommodation options and restaurants.

The railway climbs steeply uphill from Grainau, and from the base of the mountain the scenery becomes quite dramatic, with the snow-capped peaks rising above pine-forested slopes in the foothills.

The train stops at Eibsee (a lake) to enable passengers who want to do so to ride the Seilbahn Zugspitze, an aerial tramway

that operates from here to the Zugspitze summit. Extending over 3,213 m (10,541 ft), this is the world's longest free-span cable car, plus it includes the world's tallest support tower at 127 m (417 ft). It opened in 2017 to replace the original cable system that operated from 1963 until the new one opened.

In summer the lake and its surroundings are popular for swimming, boating, watersports and hiking. The Eibsee Circular Trail is popular even in winter when it is still passable. In January the lake is often completely frozen, offering a completely different

perspective. Hotel-Eibsee is located beside the lake and within walking distance of the station.

After stopping to enable passengers to alight at Eibsee Station, the cogwheel journey continues into the slopes using a series of wide curves so that the train can gain height to continue up the steep ascent.

It then arrives in Riffelriss and afterwards at the entrance to the Zugspitze Tunnel. This and the Rosi Tunnel protect the railway from extreme weather conditions. Trains pass Höllental ('Hell Valley') named after the steep-sided, narrow gorge that is an acclaimed mountaineering route which starts at Hammersbach. A kilometre short of the terminus, the underground section of the line passes almost exactly below the summit of the Zugspitze and just a few metres from the Austrian border.

The train emerges near the summit of Zugspitze with its spectacular 360-degree views, which on a clear day take in some 400 German, Austrian, Italian and Swiss peaks. The summit is right on the border with western Austria, and there are numerous winter skiing slopes radiating from Zugspitzplatt, a glacial plateau located just below the summit. Cable cars to Ehrwald (Austria) and Eibsee offer alternative access to the cogwheel railway for ascending or descending Zugspitze. The Gletscherbahn cable car from Zugspitzplatt to the summit adds another dimension to activities at the peak terminus station.

On returning to Garmisch-Partenkirchen, visitors may want to explore the possibilities of Mount Wank, which rises above the town to a height of 1,780 m (5,840 ft). The Mount Wank cable car (Wankbahn), which operates in the summer, is under the same management. Mount Wank is a destination for hikers, day-trippers and paragliders, and Wank Haus offers meals and accommodation.

ATTENTION TO DETAIL

A Zugspitze ticket enables visitors to use the cogwheel train and the Zugspitze and Gletscherbahn cable cars. The return journey can be done as a round trip on the Zugspitze cable car, on the cogwheel train or via a combination of both. The Gletscherbahn cable car can be used as often as possible throughout the day of the ticket issue.

An extension to this railway is the line from Garmisch-Partenkirchen, heading south-easterly via a pass through Mittenwald to Innsbruck in the Austrian Tyrol. This rail route of 34 km (21 miles) takes just under 90 minutes, with some 18 trains operating per day (from 6.34 a.m. to 8.20 p.m). Known as the Mittenwald Railway, it is a picturesque border crossing that operates past lakes and scenic mountainous landscapes.

The Mittenwald Railway (or Mittenwaldbahn, popularly known as the Karwendelbahn or Karwendel Railway) is a line between Innsbruck in Austria and Garmisch-Partenkirchen in Germany. It passes through Seefeld (Austria) and Mittenwald (Germany). Opened in 1912, the line was operated jointly by the Royal Bavarian State Railways and the Austrian Federal Railways. Pioneering technology meant that it substantially impacted the development of operating standards for electric railways in Central Europe.

MARIAZELL RAILWAY
STAIRWAY TO HEAVEN

The Mariazell Railway (Mariazellerbahn) from St Pölten (Sankt Pölten) in Lower Austria through to Mariazell in Styria is a railway of two parts. St Pölten to Frankenfels is known as the valley section, while that from Lauberbachmühle to Mariazell is the mountain section. The latter is a route of 30 km (18.6 miles) with 16 tunnels, seven bridges and nine viaducts.

Originally known as the Lower Austrian-Styrian Alp Railway,

the Mariazell Railway passes along a very scenic route of 91 km (36 miles) to Mariazell. This is home to a famous Roman Catholic basilica built in the fourteenth and fifteenth centuries that has been a pilgrimage site for centuries. The railway's use of *Himmelstreppe* ('Stairways to Heaven') is a reference to Mariazell Basilica. The line also provides access to numerous natural attractions, like skiing resorts in the winter and walking trails in the summer.

TRACK NOTES

A narrow-gauge railway (760 mm/2 ft 6 in long) was opened in stages between 1898 and 1907. Despite opposition, the Mariazell Railway was electrified between 1907 and 1911. The technology was considered revolutionary then, and it made use of the mountain's vast hydroelectric resources.

The service has had several operators, including ÖBB until 2010, when responsibility for the railway was transferred to the Lower Austria provincial government through its NÖVOG operations. They set about modernizing the line and its rolling stock, including purchasing low-floor Himmelstreppe Electric Multiple Units (EMUs) made by Stadler Rail of Switzerland. This also meant opening a new operational and train-storage facility at Laubenbachmühle. These EMUs typically operate at 80 km/h (50 mph).

WELCOME ABOARD

The journey from the north begins in St Pölten, Austria's oldest city, known for its Baroque and Art Nouveau architecture. The train stops at 26 stations before reaching its Mariazell terminal. There are several stations of interest, and alighting from the train to view them before joining the next train can add hours to a complete journey that takes just over two hours. The landscape is dominated by mountains, valleys and lakes, and the line traverses the valleys of rivers such as the Pielach, Nattersbach and Erlauf.

At Ober-Grafendorf, the old boiler house features restored railway infrastructure, including the famous Mh.6 steam locomotive that was manufactured in 1908. Tours are offered on weekends and public holidays from May to October.

Klangen Art Railway Station features an art gallery and sculpture park. Passengers can alight here, hire a bike and cycle along the Pielach Valley Cycle Trail. Hofstetten-Grünau Station is home to a regional museum. Mariazell Model Railway Museum adjoins Kirchberg an der Pielach Station. Frankenfels is the stop for Nix Cave, tours through the Taubenbach ravine and Hausstein Mountain Farming Museum.

Laubenbachmühle houses the operations centre of the Mariazell Railway. Puchenstuben is the station to alight at for Ötscher-Tormäuer Nature Park. Wienerbruck-Josefsberg, at the base of the Ötscher, has a Nature Park Centre from where it is possible to walk through the Ötschergräben Gorge, Lassing Waterfall and on to Erlaufklause. Gemeindealpe Mitterbach Ski Resort offers year-round mountain experiences. The chairlift takes adventurers to the 1,626 m (5,335 ft) Gemeindealpe summit for winter skiing or downhill mountain cart rides in summer.

The train terminates at Mariazell, where the impressive basilica houses an image of the Virgin Mary that is venerated by pilgrims. The station is also the terminus of the Museumstramway Mariazell-Erlaufsee, a standard-gauge heritage steam tramway that operates to the north-west and nearby Erlaufsee. The lake is a popular summer attraction, as is Holzknechtland Adventure World in nearby Bürgeralpe. With several chairlifts, Bürgeralpe is a popular mountain for winter skiing.

ATTENTION TO DETAIL

On weekdays, *Himmelstreppe* trains operate every hour between St Pölten and Laubenbachmühle. Depending on the time of year, 6–10 trains continue on to and back from Mariazell. Weekend and public holiday services are reduced, but in summer additional services are added. These include some panoramic carriages and trains hauled by historic steam locomotives. Some trains just operate from Puchenstuben and Gösling to Mariazell.

A number of the line's older electric locomotives, such as the 100-year-old Class 1099 and Class 2095 diesel locomotives, and Class 5090 diesel railcars, operate on special occasions. The Mh.6 steam engine, operated by former railway employees, does the occasional nostalgic run.

The panoramic carriage journeys that operate at weekends, public holidays and during the advent season before Christmas, offer an enjoyable journey with panoramic windows, first-class seating, and breakfast or afternoon delicacies.

Narrow-gauge trains of the Mariazellerbahn travel through the picturesque Pielach Valley.

PINZGAU LOCAL RAILWAY

A LOCAL LINE IN RURAL AUSTRIA

The narrow-gauge Pinzgauer Lokalbahn has provided a rail connection to many small communities along Austria's Upper Salzach Valley since 1898. The line has had several operators, including ÖBB, but is now operated by the provincial government. The line heads westwards from the lakeside resort town of Zell am See and heads up the Salzach River valley. The Pinzgau Valley train (Pinzgaubahn or Krimmler Bahn) operates in the Austrian province of Salzburg. The valley has been a source of salt (*salz* means salt in German), ice and copper for thousands of years.

The railway departs from the town of Zell, located beside the lake of the same name, and heads westwards for 53 km (33 miles) to its terminal station at Krimml in the Pinzgau Mountains. It provides access to many parts of the valley from its 40 stops (many are mere trackside sheds), most of which require passengers to press a buzzer in order to alight. Zell am See and the adjoining town of Kaprun are year-round resort destinations for holiday-makers, and there are numerous cultural and natural treasures nearby, including Kitzsteinhorn, Hohe Tauern National Park, the Kitzbühel Alps and the Pinzgau Grass Mountains.

The picturesque railway line from Zell am See to Wörgl via Kitzbühel (on the main Innsbruck to Salzburg line) is another regional line to consider.

TRACK NOTES

The 760 mm (2 ft 6 in) gauge line has special appeal for narrow-track railway devotees. The first train departs Zell am See at 6.30 a.m., with subsequent departures approximately every hour until 9 p.m. Normal services of three passenger carriages and a special bike transporter carriage are hauled by a diesel locomotive, and the journey takes about 80 minutes.

Floods in 2005 damaged a section of rail between Mittersill and Krimml, and it did not reopen until 2010. The line between Niedernsill and Krimml was damaged again by storms in 2021 and a bus service was introduced while repairs were carried out.

WELCOME ABOARD

Zell am See is a base for adventures on the lake and in the surrounding mountains and forests. The landmark tower of the town's Romanesque St Hippolyte Church was added in the fifteenth century. Trails and lifts lead to the skiing slopes of Schmittenhöhe Mountain. There was once a funicular railway to Gipfelwelt 3000, but that no longer operates. However, the 3K K-connection from the Maiskogel to the Kitzsteinhorn is available, and from here visitors can continue directly from Kaprun with the Gletscherjet 2 and the summit lift to the 'Top of Salzburg' viewing. The famous Grossglockner Mountain (Austria's highest peak), with its switch-back summit road and Kaiser Franz-Josefs-Höhe Glacier, is nearby.

The train passes along the Pinzgau Valley, with dairy farms extending over lush meadows and small towns dotted about. Visitor accommodation is mostly in small establishments that are popular with skiers in winter, and with hikers and cyclists in summer.

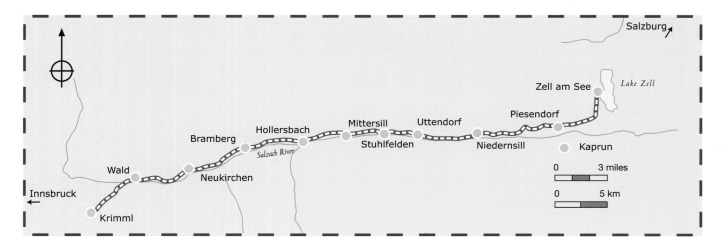

While the Pinzgau local train (Pinzgauer Lokalbahn) is used mostly by people living in the Pinzgau Valley, tourist steam trains also operate in the summer.

Stuhlfelden is typical of these small towns. Its church spire rises above the town, and family-run hotels such as the 500-year-old Schwaigerlehen and Berngarten, with just four rooms, provide personalized hospitality and hearty, home-cooked meals prepared on an ancient wooden hearth.

Mittersill provides access to Hohe Tauern National Park. Krimml Waterfalls, at 380 m (1,247 ft), are one of the highest waterfalls in Europe. The waters of the Krimmler Ache River cascade down the three-tiered, glacial-fed waterfalls located in the national park near the train terminus at Krimml. Passengers can either walk from the station or take the connecting Post Bus and complete the final walk to the base of the falls.

ATTENTION TO DETAIL

Tickets can be bought from ticket offices, the conductor or online. Guests staying in a Zell am See or Kaprun hotel can take the train for free. Most services are offered on diesel-powered locomotives, although vintage steam trains are also operated and are worth seeking out. Pre-booked reservations are essential for steam-train journeys that operate every Thursday from early July until late September, as well as during Advent just before Christmas. Steam trains run from Zell am See to Niedernsill (halfway to Mittersill) and back, a total distance of 24 km (15 miles). Food and drinks are served on board the steam trains, with a highlight being the sausages that are grilled on the steam engine's boiler. Beverages are served in the Pinzga Schenke dining car.

Bicycles can be transported on regular trains in a dedicated carriage, and many cyclists use the train to access cycling paths such as the Tauern Cycle Path, which is 67 km (42 miles) in length.

VIENNA TO TRIESTE

A CLASSIC EUROPEAN RAIL JOURNEY

This train from the Austrian capital Vienna runs to Trieste on the Adriatic Sea in north-east Italy. For a long time, Trieste was a strategic port and vital link between the Mediterranean and Central Europe. It was part of the Austro-Hungarian Empire from 1832 to 1918, with a train line first linking the two cities in 1857. The famous UNESCO-recognized Semmering Railway (page 119) forms an important section of this line that passes through parts of Austria, Slovenia and Italy.

TRACK NOTES

There are some six daily trains along the route of 348 km (216 miles), with ÖBB trains offering a direct service from Vienna to Trieste Centrale. Journeys take about eight hours and 47 minutes, but the fastest service does it in just over seven hours. These services are direct and require no change of train, although there are other trains in the respective countries for those who want to explore destinations along the way.

Austrian ÖBB is the main operator on the line, with the first train departing at 6.32 a.m. and the last at 11.35 p.m. (the second last train at 10.37 p.m. is a better option as the last train takes 13 hours to reach Trieste). Trains depart from Vienna (Wien Meidling) and arrive at Trieste Centrale. EC (including 'Emona' trains), IC, Nightjet, Railjet and Euronight trains operate on all of the track or sections of it. Railjet is ÖBB's high-speed train, which travels at speeds of up to 230 km/h (143 mph) to connect Austria's main cities with Germany, Hungary, Slovenia, Switzerland, the Czech Republic and Italy.

WELCOME ABOARD

Trains depart from Vienna Meidling Station just south-west of the capital and pass through other leading stations like Wiener Neustadt, Semmering, Bruck an der Mur, Graz, Leibnitz, Spielfeld, Maribor, Celje, Zidoni Most and Ljubljana before terminating in Trieste.

Vienna (or Wien to the locals) is arguably one of the world's most livable cities. The former capital of the Austro-Hungarian Empire is known for its landmark St Stephansdom (St Stephen's) Cathedral, Schönbrunn Palace, Imperial Habsburg Palace, Vienna Boys' Choir, museums, opera, classical composers, wine houses

in Grinzing and Advent markets. Before boarding the train to Trieste, passengers can sample superb coffee, cakes and pastries in iconic coffee houses such as Demel, Café Sacher, Café Central and Café Hawelka, or new wines of the season in a traditional Grinzing *heuriger*.

Semmering Railway between Gloggnitz and Mürzzuschlag is a highlight for train lovers and rail historians. At Bruck an der Mur, the train turns south-east from the line that heads to Klagenfurt and into northern Italy.

Graz is the next main stop and is worth exploring for passengers who want to break their journey. In Austria's second-largest city, contemporary architecture has been incorporated among its numerous heritage buildings. Graz, located on the River Mur, is an architectural trendsetter that features contemporary landmarks such as the Kunsthaus Gallery, Murinsel Island and Kastner & Öhler.

The impressive Schlossberg castle and gardens overlook the city. Visitors can take a lift or walk up 260 zigzagging steps to

admire the view, 473 m (1,552 ft) up, over Graz's red-roofed buildings.

Further down the line, Spielfeld is located near the Slovenian border with Šentilj, the first town inside Slovenia. The region straddling the Austria/Slovenia border is renowned for its wine production, with the Slovenian city of Maribor beside the River Drava set among hills covered in vineyards.

Of all the Slovenian railway stations, Zidani Most serves one of the smallest settlements along the route, but it is also one of the most scenic and strategically important. The railway station, overlooking the confluence of the Rivers Savinja and Sava, is considered one of Europe's most attractive. Zidani Most is a strategic railway junction where lines from Vienna to Ljubljana, Zagreb to Ljubljana, and Zagreb to Vienna all meet. Passengers heading to Zagreb, the Croatian capital, change trains here.

The train then pulls into Slovenia's largest city and capital, Ljubljana. The city has long been a strategic centre along a trade route that extended from the Adriatic Sea to the River Danube.

A train operated by ÖBB passing over a viaduct in Semmering, Lower Austria. After the railway arrived in 1854, Semmering developed as a summer resort town for Viennese society and later as a winter sports destination.

It came under Habsburg rule until 1918, and Ljubljana is a city with many historic landmarks, dating back to the Roman era and the Middle Ages.

Some 90 minutes later, the train arrives in Trieste on the Gulf of Trieste and the Adriatic Sea. The city is close to the Slovenian border, while Croatia is just a little further to the south. Trieste was the fourth largest city in the Habsburg Empire in 1382–1918 and has always been a strategic seaport.

ATTENTION TO DETAIL
The first Railjet/Nightjet train departs at 6.32 a.m., and the last at 10.37 p.m. Railjet trains operate by day and Nightjet trains during the evening. Railjet is ÖBB's high-speed train, which travels

at up to 230 km/h (143 mph). These trains provide services to principal destinations in Austria and its neighbouring countries.

The trains feature comfortable seating (first and second class) and modern facilities, plus designated family and quiet zones so all passengers can enjoy their journey. Leather seating in first class consists of three seats with an aisle between a two-seater and a single seat, while second class seating features six-seater compartments. Often, Austrian and Slovenian carriages are combined on one train.

Family Zone seating has a games area, a children's cinema, nappy-changing facility and storage facilities for prams. The zone is located in the last second-class carriage on Railjet trains (usually carriage 21 of 31). Quiet zones are located throughout first- and second-class carriages (usually carriage 27, 37, 23 or 33). Pre-booked tickets are less expensive than those that are bought on the day of travel.

Above and opposite The Semmering Railway is considered one of the greatest feats of railway engineering, and the high standards adopted during its construction ensure the line's continuous use up to the present day.

Top A train crossing Fleischmann Viaduct, one of the impressive sights of the UNESCO World Heritage Site Semmering Railway.

SEMMERING RAILWAY

The Semmering Railway (Semmeringbahn) operates along part of the Vienna to Trieste line between Gloggnitz and Mürzzuschlag over the Semmering in Austria. The 41 km (25 mile) railway was inscribed on UNESCO's World Heritage List in 1998, making it the first railway on the prestigious list. The line was conceived in 1841 and, when completed, was recognized for its outstanding technological solution to a major physical problem.

By 1844, railways from Vienna to Gloggnitz and from Mürzzuschlag to Graz were in place, and it became apparent that a connection between the two lines was required. Experts debated how best to overcome the saddle on Semmering Mountain.

In 1848, the railway's construction was approved, with Karl Ritter von Ghegas, a prominent Austrian railway engineer, appointed as manager. Engineers and a workforce of 20,000 had to overcome the challenging geology, steep mountains and deep ravines. So perilous was the task that 1,000 workers died from work-related deaths, as well as cholera and typhus outbreaks. They used very basic equipment and explosives to blast through the solid rock.

Ghegas also suggested an adhesion railway for Semmering's steep incline. During the construction a competition was staged to build a suitable mountain locomotive. The Austrian architect and engineer Wilhelm von Engerth was commissioned to coordinate the development of a series of Semmering locomotives.

The Semmering Railway overcame a 457 m (1,499 ft) increase in altitude (the average gradient is a remarkable 1:50). The route traverses 16 viaducts, 15 tunnels and 100 brick-arched bridges.

In October 1853 a locomotive tested the route, and on 17 July 1854 the Austrian Emperor and Empress rode along the route before it was opened to the public. It became Europe's first full-gauge mountain railway and ensured greater accessibility for the area.

On construction, the railway was considered an intelligent combination of technology and nature. It also cut the travel time from days to less than an hour. The train now takes 40 minutes to traverse some amazing natural scenery.

The design and construction were of such a high standard that very little has changed apart from the longest tunnel, the Semmering Tunnel, being rebuilt in 1952. It is now one of Austria's busiest sections of track.

A small shop at Semmering Railway Station sells books and souvenirs from Thursday to Sunday from early May to late October. Office hours are from 9 a.m. to 3.30 p.m. Groups should register ahead of time.

VIENNA TO SALZBURG

THE ROMANCE OF RAIL

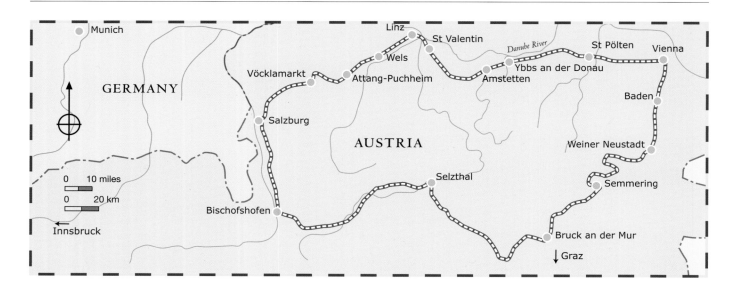

The railways from Vienna to Salzburg link two of the world's most romantic cities – the Austrian capital and the provincial capital of Salzburgerland. The railway from Vienna arrived in Linz in 1858 and was extended to Salzburg in 1860. The two cities are known for their classical composers, especially Wolfgang Amadeus Mozart, who lived in both. There are two main route options between the cities, with a direct route via Linz and a more scenic route via the famous Semmering Pass (page 119). The faster and more direct route of 251 km (156 miles) passes through St Pölten, with the possibility of combining it with the Mariazell Railway (page 112). The slower route, covering 312 km (194 miles), is more scenic but takes more than twice as long as the 150-minute direct trains.

TRACK NOTES

Both ÖBB and the privately owned WESTbahn operate on the direct route known as the Western Line. Some ÖBB trains depart from Vienna Meidling, while some other ÖBB trains and those operated by WESTbahn depart from Wien Westbahnhof (Vienna West Station). Fast, modern trains are used on both routes. Most trains have restaurant or cafe facilities.

WELCOME ABOARD

Travellers on trains from Vienna to Salzburg or vice versa are pleasantly distracted by the rich cultural histories of both cities. Both have impressive palaces, churches and Sacher Hotels, where Sachertorte and coffee are an essential Austrian experience.

City metro trains connect to Vienna Meidling and Westbahnhof Stations to provide seamless connections for trains to Salzburg. ICE, RailJet, EuroCity and S-Bahn services travel through Vienna Meidling, while Westbahnhof is a terminus for trains travelling westwards and also for WESTbahn services. Passengers joining the train in Vienna need to check which is the most appropriate to use.

While most visitors travel direct to Salzburg, it is possible to alight at stations along the way and restart the journey on a later train. Typically, WESTbahn trains from Vienna to Salzburg stop at seven stations en route – Vienna Hütteldorf, St Pölten, Amstetten, Linz, Wels, Attnang-Puchheim and Vöcklabruck – before terminating at Salzburg Station on the eastern side of the River Salzach. One of the main reasons for alighting at St Pölten is to join the narrow-gauge Mariazellerbahn, which operates through to the pilgrimage site of Mariazell.

Linz, sprawling on both sides of the River Danube, is the next stop, with the station being located on the southern bank. Its Central Railway Station is regarded as the most beautiful in Austria. This medieval trading port was briefly the imperial capital, but is now one of Austria's leading industrial cities. Cruising along the

Danube is a popular way to explore the region, with some boats heading downstream from Linz to Melk, Spitz and picturesque Dürnstein. The wines of the Wachau region are becoming increasingly popular around the globe, with many produced from grapes grown on terraces that rise above the Danube in Lower Austria.

The Pöstlingbergbahn is a narrow-gauge railway that ascends the steep incline of the Pöstlingberg in northern Linz. It departs from Main Square to the north-west of the main railway station and winds its way up the steep hill (it is one of the world's steepest railways). Its old tram carriages, dating back to 1898, add to the railway's authenticity.

Wels is an important railway junction for trains arriving from Germany via Passau to the north-west of Wels. There is also a local train from here to Grünau im Almtal, 35 km (22 miles) to the south, with the journey taking one hour.

The next junction is at Attnang-Puchheim, where it crosses the Salzkammergut Railway, which connects to Stainach-Irdning (to the south) and Ried im Innkreis (to the north-west). Afterwards, a branch line heads north from Strasswalchen through the Mattig Valley to Braunau am Inn on the border with Germany.

Above left A Railjet train operated by ÖBB crossing over the Salzach River near the main Salzburg Railway Station where trains arrive from and depart for Vienna.

Above right WESTbahn is a private Austrian railway company that provides several daily rail connections between Vienna, Salzburg and Munich.

Salzburg is regarded as one of Europe's most beautiful cities and recognized as a UNESCO World Heritage Site that protects its Old Town (Altstadt), the pedestrian shopping precinct known as Getreidegasse, Hohensalzburg Fortress and numerous churches. While not revered by Austrians, Salzburg was the setting for *The Sound of Music*, which introduced landmarks such as the Mirabell Palace and Gardens to generations of film-goers.

ATTENTION TO DETAIL

Most services offer two or three classes of travel, and tickets for all are least expensive if bought online well in advance. More expensive tickets provide greater flexibility when it comes to changing travel plans at the last minute. There are regular departures on WESTbahn and ÖBB, with tickets for the former being less expensive than those for ÖBB.

HIGH TATRAS RAILWAYS
ONE MOUNTAIN, FOUR LINES

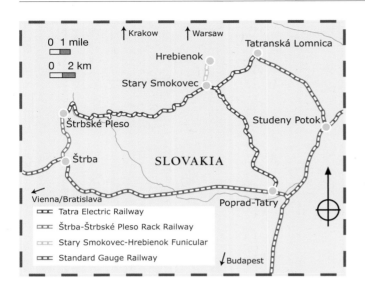

Slovakia's High Tatras (High Tatra Mountains, or Vysoké Tatry), located on the border with Poland, form the highest parts of the Carpathian Range. They are Slovakia's highest mountains and are said to be the world's smallest mountain range. Trains to the High Tatras depart from Štrba, Poprad-Tatry and Tatranská Lomnica, while Starý Smokovec serves as the network hub. Štrba and Poprad-Tatry are on the main line from Bratislava to Kŏsice.

The High Tatras, with their scenic snow-capped peaks and deep valleys, are best admired from the train, especially on a clear day. Passengers who want to travel along all four lines in the network have to backtrack on several sections. These lines, operated by OŽ and TEŽ, include the standard-gauge track (Poprad to Štrba), Tatra Electric Railway (Poprad-Tatry-Starý-Štrbské Pleso), the Hrebienok Funicular (Starý Smokovec-Tatranská Lomnica) and the Štrbské Pleso to Štrba Rack Railway.

TRACK NOTES
Various electrified trains operate on the narrow-gauge railway, including Stadler Class 495 units and the older, Stadler Class 45 EMUs. The electric units with hybrid (dual) drive eliminate the need for transfers where the two non-dependent systems currently meet. Most of the network operates on a single track, although there are some passing tracks at stations.

WELCOME ABOARD
When the Czech Republic and the Slovak Republic were created from what was previously Czechoslovakia, the former Českosloenské Státné Dráhy (Czechoslovak State Railways) was similarly divided. The České Dráhy (CD) and Žekeznice Slovenjskej Republiky (Slovak Republic Railways, or ŽSR) were set up to serve their respective countries. Although the railways are now separate, the long union between these networks and the desire to operate through-services has resulted in high levels of cooperation between both railways.

The southern terminus of the Tatra Electric Railway Southern Terminus operates from Poprad-Tatry Station, near the centre of the industrialized town of Poprad. From here, the train winds its way up to Starý Smokovec, where a change of train is required for the journey of 6 km (14 miles) up to the highest point of Tatranská Lomnica at 2,190 m (7,185 ft).

Passengers must return to Starý Smokovec and change trains for the ride of 16 km (10 miles), taking 40 minutes, to Štrbske

Pleso. Before doing so, train enthusiasts will want to take the 11-minute ride on the Hrebienok Funicular. From Hrebienok, it is possible to ride the funicular or take a walking trail back to Starý Smokovec. Although Tatranská Lomnica provides access to the highest peaks on the mountains, some of the best views are from the train that operates on the line between Starý Smokovec and Štrbské Pleso.

The western terminus of the Tatra Electric Railway is at Štrbské Pleso, which is a magical location with numerous hotels. It is a popular destination for its summer (June to September) walking trails, and challenging skiing and snowboarding in winter (December to February). The mountain is well equipped for skiers and walkers, and restaurants and hotels serve all visitors. The luxurious Grand Hotel Kempinski, near the lake, is one of the best hotels in Štrbské Pleso.

Passengers alight from the train to take the rack railway down to Štrba. This too offers stunning views along the valley. The Štrbské Pleso to Štrba rack railway runs on a 1,000 mm (3 ft 3⅜ in) gauge track that operates on a steep decline over 4.75 km (3 miles). It was built in 1896 and reconstructed in 1970 for the World Ski Championship. Štrba is located in a saddle at an elevation of 850 m (2,789 ft) above sea level.

Trains of the rack railway terminate at Štrba Railway Station, where connections are made for the trains that operate on the standard-gauge main line back to Poprad. This journey only takes 15 minutes.

ATTENTION TO DETAIL

The trains are heated in winter; they are modern and clean, and the fares are very affordable. When travelling from Tatranská Lomnica to Starý Smokovec and Štrbské Pleso, the recommended seating is by a window on the left-hand side of the train. Carriage windows are large, but there is only limited space for luggage above the seats.

Machines are located on the train, and passengers must use them to validate their tickets. First-class carriages have an aisle separating a single seat and a double seat, while in second class it is four seats across. In many cases there are tables that display route maps alongside those mounted on the wall. There are limited racks for bikes.

Opposite The Štrbské Pleso to Štrba rack railway train parked at the station.

Below One of the trains of the Tatra Electric Railway stopped at Štrbské Pleso, where passengers can admire the scenic surrounds.

TRAIN DES MERVEILLES
MEDITERRANEAN TO MARITIME ALPS

Work began on the mammoth task of constructing the Nice–Breil–Tende–Cuneo line in 1883. The engineering challenges were immense, requiring 100 viaducts and bridges in addition to tunnels and retaining walls. The line opened in 1928 and is now used by the Train des Merveilles, named after the Vallée des Merveilles (Valley of Wonders). It was partially destroyed in the Second World War and only fully reopened in 1979.

The route passes amazing scenery, ancient hilltop towns, deep gorges and some incredible railway engineering. The train heads north-east from Nice on the Côte d'Azur towards Breil-sur-Roya and the enchanting villages of La Brigue and Tende. There are many adventures to be had in Mercantour National Park, which is accessible by rail from the villages of Sospel, Breil-sur-Roya St Dalmas de Tende and Tende.

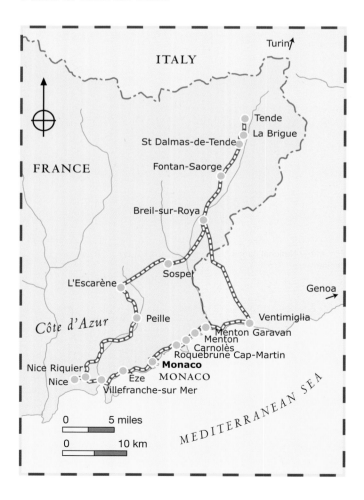

TRACK NOTES

SNCF uses Autorail à Grande Capacité (AGC) multiple-unit trains built by Bombardier. An intriguing feature of the line is the spiral tunnels that allow the train to gain altitude. Falling rocks are a problem on some of the steeper slopes, and overhead wires provide some warning and protection.

WELCOME ABOARD

Passengers can learn about the trip highlights from expert commentary (in English and French) on the 9.08 a.m. train from Nice-Ville Station (June to September and on weekends and public holidays in May and October). It is best to ask before boarding about the carriage in which the commentary can be heard. Front-facing seats are best, with the left-hand side offering the most interesting scenery. The trains are air conditioned and have over-seat luggage racks.

The train passes several villages and stops at seven before its Tende terminus. Long tunnels beneath mountains reveal remote valleys and new hilltop towns. Sospel in the Bévéra Valley has an impressive cathedral, while Breil-sur-Roya, with its beautiful station, provides access to nearby Saorge, one of France's most picturesque villages. The most impressive part of the line is between Breil-sur-Roya and the Tende Tunnel. The train pulls into Tende two hours after its departure from Nice. The fortified medieval town is home to the Musée des Merveilles, which has displays of prehistoric engravings.

Italian trains operate from Ventimiglia to Cuneo, joining the French network at Breil-sur-Roya. While a separate ticket is required for travel through Italy, a possible round trip could include travelling from Nice to Tende and, on the return, catching a Trenitalia train from Breil-sur-Roya to Ventimiglia, then a train back along the coast to Nice via Menton and Monaco. This round trip enables travel on two national railways, and the opportunity to admire Roman ruins, the city walls of medieval Ventimiglia, and its more modern and trendy coastal precincts. Its main street, Via Garibaldi, is lined with historic buildings. From this area, known to the locals as Ventimiglia Alta, visitors can take in the beautiful coastal scenery. The Lungomare, a coastal boulevard, is full of restaurants and bars that are especially popular in summer.

The train from Ventimiglia follows the coast and passes through Menton, which is home to Restaurant Mirazur, one of the most acclaimed restaurants in the world. However, train passengers wanting to dine at the three-star Michelin restaurant operated by Chef Mauro Colagreco need to make a reservation well in advance. Colagreco is also a UNESCO Goodwill Ambassador for Biodiversity and has created a cuisine that reflects his environmental values, making nature the source of inspiration for his dishes.

ATTENTION TO DETAIL
Nice is accessible from Marseille on Transport Express Régionaux (TER), which takes under three hours to reach Nice for Train Des Merveilles departures.

The Train des Merveilles passing the village of Tende, located within Mercantour National Park in the French Alps, north-east of Nice and the Mediterranean Sea.

First- and second-class tickets can be bought online or from station machines or counters. Tickets need to be punched at platform machines before travelling. A day pass enables travel on the train's network, while customers can use the tourist pass from June to September, or a 'mini-group' rate for groups of up to eight people. There are connecting Italian trains from Tende northwards to Cuneo and on to Turin.

In winter, the Train des Merveilles morphs into the Train des Neiges to provide a Nice–St-Dalmas-de-Tende service, then a bus to Castérino for cross-country skiing.

CINQUE TERRE

A RAILWAY THROUGH 'FIVE LANDS'

Cinque Terre, or 'Five Lands', is arguably one of the most picturesque coastlines in the world. The Cinque Terre National Park was gazetted in 1999 as the nation's first national park. It is also a UNESCO World Heritage Site, and has some of the most beautiful beaches along this mostly rocky and jagged coastline. Visitors can travel on the Cinque Terre Express to reach the five small villages that grip the cliffs fronting the Ligurian Sea. This fast regional train operated by Trenitalia covers the route from Levanto to La Spezia (Centrale Station) and provides access to the five Ligurian coastal villages of Monterosso (or Monterosso al Mare), Corniglia, Vernazza, Riomaggiore and Manarola.

While the 38.6 km^2 (15 mi^2) Cinque Terre National Park may be the nation's smallest national park, it is also one of its most visited. Visitors come for hiking, swimming, snorkelling, diving, sunbathing or exploring the ancient seaside towns. Organized horseback rides and mountain-biking tours are also available. The park has several hiking trails, including Sciacchetrail, which is named after the region's highly acclaimed and intensely sweet wine, called Sciacchetrà.

TRACK NOTES

The Trenitalia rapid intercity train journey to the Cinque Terre from Genoa to La Spezia is relaxing and pleasant, demonstrating that the journey is as important as the destination. Many trains that operate along the Cinque Terre route are regional trains, and the comfort and seating on them can vary. Seats cannot be reserved, but this should not be of concern to most passengers, as the journey from La Spezia to Monterosso only takes 21 minutes on average.

WELCOME ABOARD

In the past, the only way in or out of these fishing villages was via the sea. The mainline railway from either La Spezia or Genoa now provides easy access to the five coastal towns. Centuries ago Genoa was regarded as one of the most important port cities in the known world. Genoese mariners were exploring the Mediterranean and bringing back innovations, exotic goods and other treasures from around the region. Christopher Columbus grew up here, but the city's fathers and their bankrolling entrepreneurs missed a golden opportunity when they decided against funding his world explorations. Spain was more interested in Columbus's voyage to the New World and funded these. However, Columbus did depart from Genoa in 1492, and the Italians have been reminding the world of this ever since. Today, Genoa is one of the main ports of call for Mediterranean cruises.

The Sentiero Azzurro Trail (Blue Path) connects all five villages. This trail passes scenic vistas, pine forests, coastal heath, vineyards and the occasional olive grove. While some locals are still involved in fishing, agriculture and viticulture, tourism is the main money-spinner these days.

Hundreds of walkers set off every day on the well-marked path for the relaxing, six-hour coastal walk of 11 km (6.8 miles). There are some steep sections, but the trail is well formed, with numerous rest stops and the possibility of catching a train to the next station should the going get too rigorous, or if it is time to eat. Starting from the south, the first village reached is Riomaggiore. Over the centuries, the region's farmers have laboriously built some 7,000 km (4,350 miles) of stone terraces on which to farm. These steep, dry-stone terraces support vineyards that produce one of Italy's most unique and expensive sweet dessert wines, called Sciacchetrà. This luscious, dessert-style wine, produced mostly around Riomaggiore, exhibits intense dried apricot and honey flavours and is sold in half bottles at several outlets in Italy's

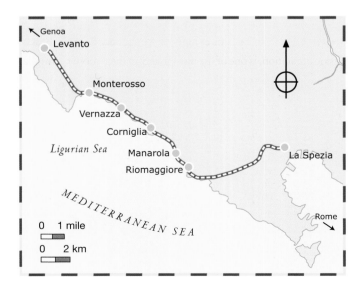

Trains stop at Manarola Station, the second smallest of the five Cinque Terre stations located along Italy's Ligurian Coast.

second-smallest wine region. Crisp, acidic white wines with a delicate bouquet are also produced from grape varieties like Bosco, Albarola and Vermentino. Red wines are made from Dolcetto and Granaccia grape varieties.

The famous Via dell'Amore (Road of Love) is the seaside hiking trail between Riomaggiore and Manarola. This path was carved into the rocky coast in the early twentieth century by workers building the railway tunnel between Riomaggiore and Manarola. Legend has it that the trail became a meeting point for lovers. Located just south of the village, Manarola Station is one of the most scenic along the coast, perched above the sea at the entrance to a tunnel. From the station, rail passengers and trail walkers have to negotiate Scalinata Lardarina, a winding staircase that leads to the hamlet. There are numerous vantage points for photography on the stairway, with Manarola's colourful houses and its San Lorenzo Church forming a picturesque backdrop.

Much of the rail journey to Corniglia is done through a tunnel. The line re-emerges at Corniglia Station, with its uninterrupted coastal views and the hamlet high above the sea. Guvano Beach, beside the station, is one of the most lovely in the region. Corniglia, perched on a ridge high above the Ligurian Sea, is the smallest of the five villages. It is home to the fourteenth-century Church of San Pietro, and coastal views are best seen from the Belvedere viewpoint.

Car-free Vernazza is the next village along the route. Like Riomaggiore, Vernazza has a small but beautiful harbour lined with colourful fishing boats. It has the only natural port of the five Cinque Terre ports and is also home to Castello dei Doria, an ancient fort. The village's name originates from the indigenous wine called Vernaccia, which is not to be confused with the more famous Tuscan white wine, Vernaccia di San Gimignano.

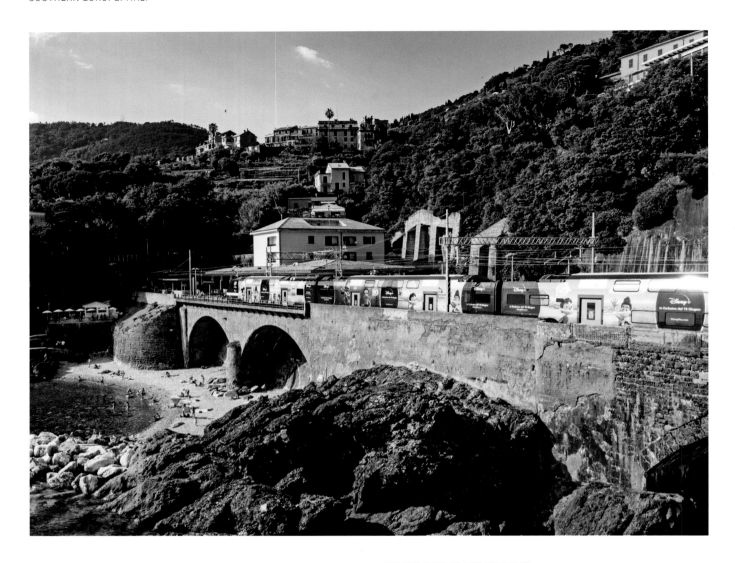

Monterosso is the most populous and westernmost village. It is fronted by Fegina Beach, the most famous along the Cinque Terre. Its sandy expanse stands out among the mostly rocky beaches of the Ligurian Riviera. Passengers virtually step from the train on to the sandy beachfront, which is lined with bars, restaurants, several gelato parlours and boutique hotels. Built on the ruins of an ancient pre-Roman settlement, the village dates to the ninth century. Its small stretch of yellow sand is popular, especially in summer, when it gets quite crowded.

The town is divided in two parts marked by the medieval tower of Aurora. Its old town is dominated by the castle ruins and characterized by narrow medieval streets, with colourful terraced houses, restaurants, cafes and shops. Interested visitors should plan their visit around the Farmer's Market staged every Thursday morning or in late May for Sagra dei Limoni or the Lemon Festival.

ATTENTION TO DETAIL

Liguria is known for its exceptional coastal scenery, but accessibility is difficult, with the train providing the perfect solution. The key access stations of Genoa (Genova) and La Spezia are linked to rail services operated by Trenitalia and Italo high-speed services. Cinque Terre Express regional trains depart from La Spezia and Levanto every 30 minutes during daylight hours. However, peak-season Trenitalia services from late March until early November provide 99 train journeys, which operate every 15 minutes throughout the day. The complete journey along the Cinque Terre from La Spezia to Monterosso takes 21 minutes, with the first train departing at 4.30 a.m. and the last at 1 a.m. Trains from Genoa to La Spezia take 95 minutes, with the first departure at 5.10 a.m. and the last at midnight. These trains depart from Genoa Brignole, a few kilometres by train from the main

Genoa Railway Station. The five Cinque Terre stations are just minutes apart by train.

Narrow streets and lanes are a feature of most of the villages, but it is almost impossible to get lost. Maps in various languages are available from the park's ticket offices, but the main trail is easy to follow. Visitors to the national park, or any of its five towns, need to buy a park-entry ticket. Those planning to travel to any of the five towns from a station outside the national park have to pay a supplement. Children aged 4–11 years travel for half price, and those under four travel for free. Tickets need to be validated before departure and are valid for 75 minutes and for only one route (intermediate stops are not allowed).

Most visitors who walk along the Cinque Terre do it once, and it is not unknown for some restaurateurs to charge a premium for often mediocre fare. However, many walkers are distracted

Above An enclosed pedestrian tunnel from Riomaggiore Railway Station, running parallel to the rail track provides access to the lower part of a stream that runs through it into the tranquil waters of Ligurian Sea.

Opposite Passengers who travel to the Cinque Terre from Genoa by train will pass through seaside towns like Framura where beaches for sunbathing are located immediately adjacent to the railway platforms.

by the magical views and the enticing local wines, and overlook any culinary shortcomings.

The Cinque Terre will appeal to rail travellers who like to combine an exciting coastal rail journey, culture and history with healthy outdoor activity. While it is possible to combine walking with journeys on the train, a good approach would be to walk the entire route in the morning, have lunch or a swim, then catch the train back to the starting-point station.

TRENINO VERDE

RIDE THE LITTLE GREEN TRAINS

Trenino Verde, or 'little train', is used to describe the smaller trains that operate along several narrow-gauge lines on the Italian island of Sardinia. Located in the Tyrrhenian Sea, Sardinia lies south of Corsica and just off the west coast of Italy. Its reference to 'green' is not due to the train's colour, but rather to the green heart of the island that several trains pass through. The island, which covers 8,722 km² (3,368 mi²), is well serviced by various train routes.

Sardinia is a popular destination for those who seek an island holiday by the beach, but this is complemented by its train network that provides access to the mountainous interior. Its trains journeys are characterized by authenticity and slowness, and appeal especially to those seeking a nostalgic rail experience.

Trains on the island are operated by either Trenitalia or the Little Green Train. The latter is the railway service managed and promoted by the former Ferrovie della Sardegna, which is now named ARST SpA. Having been in operation for more than 130 years, these rail services provide a journey back in time.

The principal line through Sardinia is the north–south route from Porto Torres to Cagliari via Oristano. Some trains only operate during the summer tourist season (mid-June to mid-September), with a popular route from Arbatax on the east coast, south-west to Mandas in the island's interior, and from here to either Sorgono (north) or Cagliari (south). The train heading from Mandas to Sorgona passes through untouched woodland on its journey to Laconi. The Sassari to Tempio Pausania and Palau rail route has been used exclusively by and for the Trenino Verde tourist service since 2015.

TRACK NOTES

Most routes are on a single track, so delays may occur as one train waits for the other to clear the track. Patience is something that passengers need on these trains, as there can be unexpected delays.

Trains operating on the lines include the Ade and Adm diesel-powered rail cars (with 55 seats), Lde diesel locomotives, V2d model carriages (with 72 seats), and a Breda steam locomotive.

Breda was an Italian manufacturer of steam locomotives established in Milan in 1886. Over 100 Breda locomotives are displayed in parks and at stations mostly in Italy but also in Greece, Eritrea, Denmark, the Netherlands and South Africa.

WELCOME ABOARD

Some coaches dating back to 1913 have wooden benches, and the windows can be left open for uninterrupted photography. Passengers should not be too surprised if the conductor hops out to chase sheep from the track or to stop traffic at level crossings. While trains operated by Trenino Verde may be slow, few passengers appear to complain. Extended stops are made for passengers to have an espresso or use a toilet.

One of the more exciting journeys is the route of 62 km (39 miles) from the marina port of Arbatax inwards to Gairo. This journey starts midway down the east coast and takes three and a half hours to reach its destination. It slowly winds its way into the interior and passes through the mountain villages of Elini and

A diesel-electric railcar operated as the Little Green Train travelling from Mandas to Laconi on the Italian island of Sardinia.

Lanusei, and past Lago Alto del Flumendosa. Lanusei is perched on top of Gennargentu Ridges, with views down to the coast, and Selene Forest, with its rich stands of ilex and oak trees, is nearby. The train arrives in Gairo Taquisara, where it is possible to visit the ghost villages of Osini Vecchio and Gairo Vecchio. The original villages date back to the fourteenth century, but a severe flood in 1951 left many of the buildings in an unstable and unusable state, and the decision was made to relocate both villages. The relocation was completed in 1969, and now the ghost villages are popular tourist sites.

The old village, Gairo Vecchio, is 2 km (1.2 miles) south of the new Gairo Taquisara. It is one of the most famous abandoned places in Sardinia and in Italy.

ATTENTION TO DETAIL

According to the operators of Trenino Verde, it has the longest tourist railway network in Europe (434 km/271 miles). It operates scheduled services along sections of Sardinia's rail network. These include Isili to Sorgono (83 km/52 miles), Mandas to Arbatax (159 km/99 miles), Macomer to Bosa Marina (46 km/29 miles), and Nulvi to Palau via Tempio (116 km/72 miles).

Railway museums also operate on premises adjacent to both Monserrato and Tempio Pausania Railway Stations, but it is best to check whether these are open.

Sadly, several lines on the island have closed, but tourism is helping to keep the remaining lines viable for future generations to experience.

FLORENCE TO NAPLES

A FAST & EFFICIENT CLASSIC JOURNEY

The rail journey on high-speed rail between Florence (Firenze) and Naples (Napoli) is fast and affordable. Train passengers can choose between travelling on the state-owned Trenitalia and the privately owned Italo Treno. Trenitalia operates the high-speed trains known as Frecciarossa (Frecce), plus the slower Frecciabianca and intercity tilting trains referred to as Frecciargento. The latter operate on traditional lines outside the high-speed network.

TRACK NOTES

The Frecciarossa (red arrow) fleet includes the Frecciarossa 1000, which can travel at a top speed of 400 km/h (249 miles), and the Frecciarossa ETR 500, which can attain a top speed of 300 km/h (186 mph). Development of the trains began in 2008 as a joint venture between multinational conglomerate Alstom and Italian rail manufacturer Hitachi Rail Italy. One of the conditions of its development was that it needed to be capable of travelling on rail tracks in Austria, Belgium, France, Germany, the Netherlands, Spain and Switzerland. Trains entered commercial service in June 2015, just in time for the Milan Expo.

WELCOME ABOARD

This journey commences in Florence (Firenze) and heads southwards past the capital Rome and on to the Mediterranean Sea city of Naples. The Tuscan capital of Florence is the cradle and heart of the Renaissance and a popular city to visit while in Italy. The city's older precincts of narrow, cobbled streets lead on to expansive plazas, and church spires rise high above the terracotta-tiled rooflines. Several days should be allocated to explore its world-class museums and art galleries, while the stately buildings lining both sides of the River Arno have important heritage value. Visitors are drawn to the thirteenth-century Church of Santa Maria Novella, after which the railway station is named. Other city highlights include Michelangelo's statue of *David* at the Galleria dell'Accademia, the Uffizi Galleries, the Il Duomo (the Cathedral of Santa Maria dei Fiori), the Palazzo Vecchio, the Palazzo Pitti and the famous bridge, the Il Ponte Vecchio.

Both railway stations in Florence are located on the northern side of the River Arno, just to the north of the historic inner-city precinct. Firenze Santa Maria Novella (Firenze SMN), built in 1848, is the main station, although the current building only dates back to 1934. Trenitalia and Italo Treno operate trains from both Santa Maria Novella Station and the nearby Firenze Campo Marte Station, so it is important to check in at the correct location. There are regular departures from both stations to Naples Central Station (Napoli Centrale). The journey takes nearly three to three and a half hours, depending on the type of train.

Visitors who fly into Aeroporto di Firenze-Peretola can travel via light rail (T2 Vespucci Line) to Novella, close to Florence's main railway station, to board a train to Rome, Naples, and other parts of Italy and Europe. Florence's T1 Leonardo Line runs at 90 degrees to the T2 Line, but also provides access to the railway station.

Florence makes a great rail base for exploring some other Tuscan destinations, including Livorno, Pisa and Siena. The latter is a popular day trip, and there are up to 16 daily regional trains travelling along the route of 85.5 km (53 miles), which takes 90 minutes. Hourly departures provide good connectivity and

An Italo ETR675 Pendolino high-speed train passing some of Tuscany's famous vineyards best known for producing Chianti.

reservations are not required, but tickets need to be validated before boarding the train.

Trains heading south pass some impressive Tuscan countryside, with a landscape dominated by vineyards and hilltop fortress towns. While the train does not provide immediate access to the renowned wine regions of Chianti, San Gimignano, Montalcino and Montepulciano, dedicated wine connoisseurs can use the local train, bus and car connections from Florence to sample the fruits of the vines.

Passengers are updated on the train's progress, its speed and the next station from ceiling-mounted information screens. These are also fitted in the back of each seat in all classes. As well as the speed, the screens show the location of the train on a map, the next stop, the estimated time of arrival at the next station and the weather. A camera positioned at the front of the train provides coverage of the journey as it rapidly passes along the route.

The rail journey to Rome is 233 km (145 miles), while to Naples it is an additional 189 km (117 miles). The high-speed train from Florence to Rome takes just 90 minutes, while Naples to the south takes a similar time.

Passengers travelling from Rome to Florence can join the train at Rome's Stazione Termini (the capital's main station) or Stazione Tiburtina. Visitors arriving at Rome's Fiumicino Airport can travel continuously from the airport to Florence (and vice versa) without changing trains.

The train pulls into Naples Central Station, located within walking distance of the bustling harbour. The port city offers many attractions, including churches, museums, catacombs, chapels

Right Rail passengers travelling between Florence and Naples should allocate time to explore the numerous tourist attractions in both cities, especially the famous Duomo, a Renaissance landmark in Florence.

Opposite top Santa Maria Novella Station (pictured) is close to the historic centre of Florence ,while Napoli Centrale is Naples' biggest station and a hub for city and regional buses plus the Naples Metro.

Opposite bottom High-speed trains from Florence to Naples cover the distance in around three hours.

and castles. The famous archaeological sites of Pompeii and Herculaneum are located to the south of the city at the base of Mount Vesuvius, which famously erupted in 79 .
The volcano, offshore islands and the Sorrento Peninsula are visible from Castel Sant'Elmo, perched above the notoriously narrow alleyways of Quartieri Spagnoli (Spanish Quarter) near the city centre. A stroll along the Lungomare Caracciolo coastal boulevard is another essential activity, along with sampling pizza from the town where it was created.

ATTENTION TO DETAIL

The high-speed trains are modern, clean, and offer food and beverages for purchase during the trip (passengers can also bring their own on board). Frecciarossa trains offer four classes: Standard, Premium, Business and Executive.

There are three classes on Italo Treno: Smart (second class), Prima (first class) and Club (premium first class).

Tickets on both railways between Florence and Naples can be bought online months in advance, or secured at the train station a few minutes before departure. The general rule is that the earlier the purchase, the lower the price, sometimes by 50 per cent. Travellers on a budget should avoid travelling on peak-hour and peak-season trains. Ticket prices for early morning, around noon and evening services are mostly lower due to lower demand. Weekend and public holiday services are typically less frequent and occasionally take longer than weekday services. Tickets can be bought at ticket stands and ticket machines inside any station, and need to be validated on the platform before boarding the train. Most high-speed train operators offer discounts for return travel on the same day. Schedules vary depending on the time of year and the day of the week (trains are less frequent on Sundays).

All passengers have facilities like foldaway tables, USB ports, Wi-Fi and power points. Executive class seating is more comfortable and spacious than that in other classes, and includes 10 large, rotatable chairs that swivel 180 degrees. Reading lights, a reclining backrest, and a footrest that is controlled by in-seat buttons are added extras. A dedicated meeting room for five passengers around a large table is also available. Passengers in this part of the train can have complimentary meals and beverages (including alcohol) from three menus. Other passengers have access to the FRECCIABistró located in the middle carriage of most trains.

Slower regional trains on the 'classic' route can take three and a half to four and a half hours to cover the distance. The faster trains pass directly along the line, while the slower trains often require a change of trains at places like Empoli. The slower trains are also older and offer fewer comforts than the modern, faster trains. The prices for regional train tickets rarely fluctuate and are valid on a range of dates and times. Regional trains have no food service or cafe cars.

PORTUGAL
DOURO LINE

A JOURNEY THROUGH TERRACED VINEYARDS

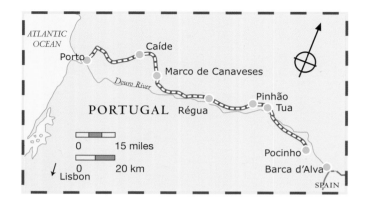

The train along the Douro Valley provides access to some of the most spectacular, picturesque and isolated vineyards in the world, best known for their famous Ports. The region is also becoming increasingly well known for its red and white wines, mostly produced from endemic grape varieties.

The scenic railway operated by Comboios de Portugal (CP) passes through the challenging riverine landscape of the Douro Valley. The journey from Porto (Oporto) to Pocinho in the Alto Douro extends over a distance of 175 km (109 miles), and takes up to three and a half hours to complete from start to finish, with a change of trains at Marco de Carnaveses for some services. While most trains terminate at the village of Pocinho, some stop at either Pinhão or Régua (also known as Peso da Régua). There has been some discussion about reopening the line of 28 km (17 miles) from Pocinho to Barca d'Alva on the border with Spain (the line was closed in 1988). The railway extended to Salamanca, Spain, until 1984.

Work on the line began in 1875 and reached Penafiel later that year. The line was completed in late 1887 with the opening of the section to Barca d'Alva and La Fregeneda. The last narrow-track feeder line disappeared when the Tua Line (Tua to Cachão) closed in 2008. The Corgo Line (Régua to Vila Real) and the Tâmega Line (Livração to Amarante) were closed in 2009.

While boats travel along the picturesque Douro, train enthusiasts prefer to choose the train journey as it provides access to the stunning scenery beyond Pinhão. Most boats terminate at the Port-producing village of Pinhão, but the railway continues further upstream past impressive rock walls and beautiful *quintas*, or wine estates. Some estates also operate retail outlets in Porto.

TRACK NOTES

In the 1990s, the Douro Line underwent extensive modernization in the district of Porto, aimed at duplicating and electrifying the track. This enabled improvements to the services provided, but it is a single track with diesel-powered railcars from Caide. Series 592 railcars are used on a route that crosses 35 bridges and viaducts and passes through 23 tunnels.

Classic trains operated by CP to Pocinho consist of Sorefame (second series), Corail or Schindler carriages. These are normally hauled by 1400 Series locomotives dating to the 1960s.

WELCOME ABOARD

The Douro Line, which starts in atmospheric Porto (at either Porto São Bento or Porto Campanhã Stations), is considered one of Portugal's most beautiful railways. Using train and boat services can maximize the Douro experience. The recommended journey is to take the train to Pinhão, the boat to Tua at the confluence of the Douro and Tua Rivers, and then rejoin the train to Pocinho.

Porto has a lively nightlife, with bars and restaurants serving the fruits of the Douro vines situated along the waterfront. The line, for a large part of its route, follows the northern bank of the River Douro, which includes Portugal's longest stretch of water-lined railway. The main purpose of the railway was, in addition to providing access for villagers, to transport supplies and products in and out of the valley. The most important export is wine, especially Port, the highly prized fortified wine made famous in the valley by estates like Symington, Niepoort, Dow's and Croft.

The initial hour of the journey, through Ermesinde, Caide and Marco de Carnaveses Stations, is mostly residential and uninspiring. Peso do Régua (Régua) is home to three bridges and the Museu do Douro. The museum provides information on the history and traditions of the region. The scenery, dominated by towering gorges, is more interesting beyond Régua.

Both Régua and Pinhão have charming riverfronts, and the latter has one of Europe's most scenic railway stations, decorated in distinctive blue and white *azulejos* mosaic tiles. The scenery from Pinhão to Pocinho is some of Europe's most picturesque, with steep slopes blanketed in vineyards rising above the River Douro. The line clings to the precipitous slopes, making for an exhilarating ride. The upper Douro is on UNESCO's World Heritage List, and more can be learnt about the railway in the museum at Tua Station.

Pocinho is the end of the line for now unless plans to reactivate it are implemented. The prehistoric rock art in the Vale do Côa, just south of the town, is the main reason to linger in the town. Returning to Tua, Régua or Pinhão makes more sense for those who want to stay overnight in the Douro.

ATTENTION TO DETAIL

Three classes are offered on the journey, with even the basic bench seats providing reasonable comfort. Choose a seat on the right-hand side of the train to Régua, but be prepared to change seats on the way to Pocinho to fully appreciate the views. Historic tourist trains occasionally operate along the line between Régua and Tua, with steam locomotive 186 used for these rail excursions.

Children three years of age and below travel for free as long as they do not occupy a seat, while those between four and twelve travel at 50 per cent of the adult fare but are allocated a seat. Senior citizens and pensioners are also entitled to a discount.

LISBON TO LAGOS

GATEWAY TO THE ALGARVE

The Comboios de Portugal (CP) premium rail service from Lisbon (Lisboa) to Lagos in the south of Portugal provides a fast and very relaxing way to travel between the capital and one of the most popular destinations along the Algarve coast. Situated at the mouth of the River Bensafrim, Lagos has a long maritime history dating back 2,000 years. It was a base for Henry the Navigator in an era when Portuguese explorers and mariners dominated global exploration. The more famous Lagos in Nigeria may have been named after the city, as it was frequented by Portuguese mariners as far back as the fifteenth century. While this Portuguese town along the Algarve coast facing the Atlantic Ocean is only home to some 33,000 permanent residents, its numbers grow considerably during summer as holidaymakers flock to its beaches, recreational facilities, tourist attractions and wineries.

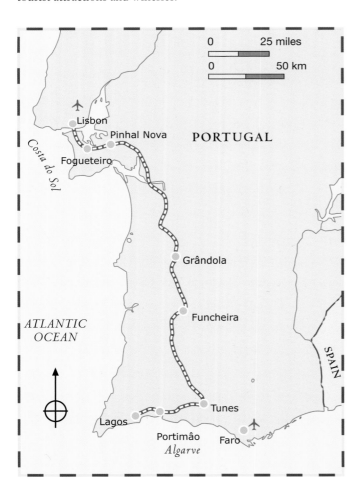

Trains on the line of 318 km (198 miles) from Lisbon to Lagos are operated by the national rail operator, CP. The railway provides regular services ranging from high-speed (Lisbon to Tunes) to local trains (Tunes to Lagos) with the latter stopping more frequently at intermediary railway stations.

The line from Lisbon to Lagos now forms part of the longest continuous railway in the world. This route extends from southern Portugal, eastwards across Europe and Asia, and all the way to the island state of Singapore (page 141).

TRACK NOTES

The electrified Lisbon to Faro route is used by various types of train, including Portugal's finest, the Alfa Pendular (AP) high-speed trains. AP trains are rapid, tilting trains that can change the lean of the carriages, tilting them towards a curve to provide a smoother ride for passengers. The technology enables trains to travel through bends much faster than regular trains. AP trains entered service with CP in 1999, and while they are assembled in Portugal, they are Italian in design and part of the Pendolino portfolio of tilting trains. These trains are designed by the rail division of car manufacturer Fiat. They are not only fast but also have stylish interiors that were recently refurbished and modernized. AP trains can travel at speeds of up to 220 km/h (140 mph).

WELCOME ABOARD

The train service from Lisbon to the Algarve has dramatically improved over the past few years. All trains on the route provide excellent facilities such as spacious seating, luggage areas, Wi-Fi and in-seat power sockets. Premier AP trains offer Comfort (Conforto) and Tourist (Turistica) Classes, with the former including access to the CP Lounge at Lisbon Estação do Oriente Station, a welcome kit (newspaper/magazine and earphones), three seats across the carriage, and an in-seat meal/beverage. Tourist Class seating is four across the carriage, and passengers have access to the cafe car.

Travellers arriving in Lisbon by plane can connect directly from the airport to this railway via a short metro line that departs from Terminal One. The metro provides access to Lisbon Estação do Oriente, Portugal's busiest railway station. This grand station,

built for Expo '98, showcases modernist architecture.

Before heading to the Algarve, travellers should allocate time to ride on Lisbon's iconic trams, operated by Carris. Most visitors choose the historic yellow Remodelado trams, but the modern Siemens Articulado trams have their own charm and operate in the flatter parts of the network. The most famous tram route is the 4.4 km (2.7 mile) E28 from Martim Moniz to Campo de Ourique. It is noteworthy because it utilizes the older and most famous heritage trams and passes through Lisbon's historic and cultural heartland. The downside is that the route is popular with tourists, and it is best to ride these trams as early as possible to avoid crowds.

Passengers can join the southbound train at either Estação do Oriente or Entrecampos Stations on its journey via the Ponte 25 de Abril suspension bridge across the River Tagus. Previously, passengers had to use a ferry service between Barreiro and central Lisbon.

Stops along the Lagos route could include Pragal, Pinhal Nova, Grândola, Ermidas-Sado, Funcheira, Ermidas-Sado, Tunes, Silves and Portimão. Trains pass through a scenic landscape of farmland, orchards, forests (including cork trees), vineyards and olive groves.

Depending on the AP or IC service, passengers have to change trains at Tunes for connecting services to Lagos. Tunes, 259 km

Comboios de Portugal (CP) operates Alfa Pendular (AP) high-speed trains with tilting capabilities.

(161 miles) south of Lisbon, is the main junction for trains heading westwards to Lagos, situated at the end of the line. The main line continues from Tunes to the south-east for Albufeira, Faro, Tavira and Vila Real de Santo António. The regional service from Tunes to Lagos is slower and passes through Algoz, Silves and Portimão, where it crosses the River Arade. Just before terminating at Lagos Station, trains travel past the expansive beachfront of Meia Praia. Lagos Station is the western terminus of the Linha do Algarve line, which connects Lagos to Vila Real de Santo António (via Faro and Tavira) in the east.

The old port of Lagos played a crucial role in Portugal's Age of Discovery and has a fascinating maritime history. Its old buildings include fortified walls, Castelo de Lagos and the impressive Santa Maria Church, dating back to the fifteenth century. Visitors can learn more about the town's strategic historical importance and seafaring traditions at the Centro de Ciência Viva de Lagos.

The Algarve has one of Europe's most alluring coastlines and its tourist destinations welcome millions of sun-worshipping holidaymakers annually. Its population triples during the summer as tourists flock here to enjoy a seaside holiday, along with cycling, hiking, watersports and horse riding. One of the town's most prized viewpoints is from the Ponta da Piedade headland. Its old streets are lined with laid-back restaurants offering fresh seafood such as local specialties of octopus, fish and clams. Dishes such as *conquilhas à Algarvia* (small clams sautéed in olive oil and garlic) and *cataplana de marisco* (mixed seafood cooked in wine) are eagerly devoured. Wines are produced in the region, and visiting wineries is another activity that appeals to visitors.

ATTENTION TO DETAIL

Timetables are available on CP's website, and tickets can be booked directly via the site. Three types of train, Alfa Pendular (AP), Intercidades (IC) and Regional, service the route, and all offer first- and second-class seating. AP high-speed trains provide the fastest service, while regional trains are the slowest. There are currently two daily departures for AP services (connecting Oporto in the north of Portugal to Faro in the Algarve via Lisbon), three

IC and several regional services. Journeys take 218–256 minutes to reach Lagos with either one or two intermediary stops. The main change of train occurs at Tunes.

Seat reservations on AP and IC long-distance trains from Lagos to Lisbon or Porto are compulsory. These trains are busiest from Lisbon on Friday evenings, Sunday evenings and public holidays.

It is also possible to travel from Spain to Lagos on an overland journey that combines train and bus. Such a journey commences by bus from the impressive Santa Justa Station (Spain) to Faro (Portugal) and takes 150–190 minutes. Buses depart from the station every few hours, and Spanish rail operator Renfe sells combined rail/bus tickets.

Lisbon Estação do Oriente or Lisbon Orient Station, one of the city's main transport hubs, was designed by the Spanish architect Santiago Calatrava and completed in 1998 for Expo '98.

THE WORLD'S LONGEST RAILWAY JOURNEY

The route of 18,755 km (11,654 miles) from Lagos (Portugal) to Singapore is the longest continuous rail journey in the world. The recently opened stretch of track, 406 km (252 miles) in length, through Lao PDR (Laos) provided the missing link in the continuous rail connectivity from South-east Asia to Europe. At its southern end, the Chinese-built, high-speed Lao PDR railway connects to the State Railway of Thailand network at Nong Khai on the River Mekong. At this line's northern end, the China-Laos Railway crosses the Lao PDR/China border at Boten (Lao PDR)/Mohan (China). From here, the Chinese railway proceeds northwards to Kunming and from there, a continuous rail track extends to Lagos (Portugal).

This journey involves numerous changes of trains and non-stop travel that has been timed to take a minimum of 21 days to complete. The epic journey passes through 13 countries – Portugal, Spain, France, Germany, Poland, Belarus, Russia, Mongolia, China, Lao PDR, Thailand, Malaysia and Singapore. The geopolitical situation in some countries along this route may result in trains not always operating, but at least the line is in place for when these situations stabilize.

Previous rail routes involved travelling on the Trans-Siberian Express across Russia, through Mongolia and China, to southern Vietnam. However, there was a gap in the railway between Ho Chi Minh City and Phnom Penh (Cambodia) because a rail track had never been laid. The new route through Lao PDR eliminates travelling through Cambodia and Vietnam.

Chinese-built trains like this one parked at Vientiane Railway Station in Laos now enable a continuous rail journey from Singapore to Lagos.

Some other remote, long and continuous rail-passenger journeys from Singapore could include to Britain's westernmost railway station of Arisaig on Scotland's West Highland Line (page 52), or Europe's northernmost railway station of Narvik in the Arctic Circle region of Norway.

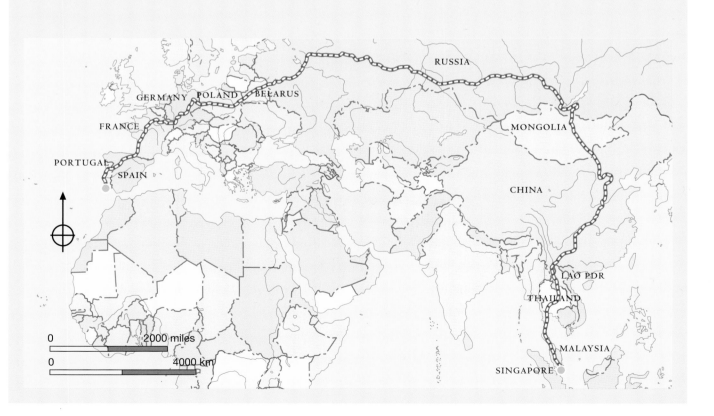

141

MADRID TO MÁLAGA

SPAIN'S AVE HIGH-SPEED TRAINS

Spain's national railway operator, Renfe-Operadora (Renfe), has some of the world's fastest trains on its AVE (Alta Velocidad Española) network. Its high-speed rail network is Europe's longest, with 3,622 km (2,251 miles) of track, and the world's second longest after China. The countries that pioneered high-speed rail technology have taken great national pride in their trains. Japan's Shinkansen is the most famous, followed by the French Train à Grande Vitesse (TGV). By contrast, some countries have been content to import and adapt high-speed technology to accommodate their own situations and needs. Spain has done a little of both.

Spain developed and promoted advanced train technology with the TALGO system (Tren Articulado Ligero Goicoechea Oriol, which was named after its two founders), while also importing high-speed trains from Germany and France. In 2005 Renfe introduced its 102 series, a train manufactured by TALGO, and the first high-speed train designed entirely in Spain and capable of speeds of up to 330 km/h (205 mph). TALGO was originally conceived as a lightweight train with a low centre of gravity, but the system has been further refined as a passive tilting train to enable greater speeds through curves by reducing the effects of

centrifugal forces on passengers. More recently, it has adopted gauge-changing technology.

In the 1990s, Spain imported the French high-speed system, and it built new high-speed lines to connect its main cities. These initially accommodated specially styled TGV-like trains marketed as Alta Velocidad Española (AVE) and gauge-changing TALGO units marketed under several names, including Avant and Avala.

The first AVE route opened in 1992, connecting Madrid, Córdoba and Seville (Sevilla). Its success led to an expansion of the network, with the Madrid to Málaga and Madrid to Valladolid AVE routes opening in 2007, Madrid to Barcelona in 2008, and Madrid to Valencia in 2011. The tourism revival in parts of Spain has been attributed to high-speed rail.

TRACK NOTES

The bulk of the Spanish railway network uses a broad-gauge track (1,676 mm/5 ft 6 in), while most European networks use standard gauge (1,435 mm/4 ft 8½ in), which was established in Britain in

the 1820s. However, Spain's newly built high-speed lines use the more common standard gauge. This enables direct connections to neighbouring countries through the link to the French network at the Perthus Tunnel (opened in 2013 beneath the Eastern Pyrenees, connecting Figueres to Perpignan).

Very fast AVE services operate between Madrid and Málaga at half-hourly intervals. With a top speed of 300 km/h (186 mph), most AVE trains are scheduled to cover 470 km (292 miles) in just two and a half hours. The ride is smooth, as the Spanish railway network is one of the finest in the world.

Among the most modern Spanish high-speed train sets are TALGO-Bombardier-built units, colloquially known as 'Pato' (duck) because of their pronounced duckbill-styled front end. In addition to these 300 km/h (186 mph) trains, TALGO gauge-changing trains that travel at more moderate speeds allow fast through services to take advantage of the existing Iberian-gauge network, and thus they serve a host of destinations beyond the high-speed lines.

Above Alta Velocidad Española or AVE trains similar to this are operated by Renfe on the rail line between Madrid and Málaga.

Opposite The Spanish high-speed rail network, on part of which the AVE services like those from Madrid to Málaga operate, is Europe's longest and the second longest in the world, after China.

In 2021, the new low-cost AVE, or Avlo, began operations between Madrid, Zaragoza, Barcelona and Figueres and, since 2022, between Madrid, Cuenca, Requena and Valencia. This made high-speed travel more accessible to those travelling on a budget.

WELCOME ABOARD

AVE trains depart from Madrid's Puerta de Atocha Station and mostly travel non-stop to terminate at Málaga-María Zambrano Station, fronting the Alboran Sea. Trains from Madrid to Málaga (along with those to Alicante and Almeria) enable ferry connections to Morocco and Algeria in North Africa. Southern lines to Málaga also provide access to Ciudad Real, Puertollano, Córdoba, then either Seville/Cádiz or Puente Genil, Antequera and Granada or Málaga. These stops are accessible by mid-distance, high-speed trains such as Avant and Avala.

One hour into the journey, trains pull into Ciudad Real. Some 47 minutes later, the AVE arrives in Córdoba, in Andalusia. Located on the River Guadalquivir, the historic city is one of Spain's most popular tourist sites, with its distinctive Moorish architecture, especially the UNESCO World Heritage Site of the Mezquita. There are three other UNESCO sites in and around the city, giving it the highest concentration of any location in the world.

From Córdoba passengers can travel to the south-west and Seville, or due south to Málaga via Puente Genil and Antequera. The train takes just less than an hour to reach Málaga.

Just beyond Córdoba trains pass the impressive Castillo de Almodóvar, immediately adjacent to the tracks. Passengers can disembark at Antequera for the high-speed service to Granada, with its famous Alhambra Moorish fortress – now protected as a UNESCO World Heritage Site.

Málaga is located on the Costa del Sol and is a popular year-round tourist town. Different civilizations have left their mark on the varied architectural styles of the city and region. It was the birthplace of Pablo Picasso, and a museum celebrating his life and art is a popular tourist attraction, as is Alcazaba Castle.

Other regional trains (including Alvia and Altaria services) operate alongside or adjacent to the AVE track, enabling passengers to alight or board at stations between the main stops. There are various commuter trains from Málaga to different parts of the Costa del Sol. One such service operates westwards, taking 50 minutes to reach its terminus at Fuengirola.

ATTENTION TO DETAIL

The railway's schedule is guaranteed, and if an AVE train runs more than 15 minutes late passengers get a partial refund, while they get a full refund if the train is more than 30 minutes late. However, the timekeeping is good, so very few refunds are made. There are three types of fare sold on AVE trains: Basic (Básico), Choose (Elige) and Premium (Prémium). Basic is the cheapest but the least flexible, and tickets are mostly purchased for last-minute trips when there is no uncertainty about the trip. Tickets known as Choose are flexible (allowing a free change and 70 per cent refund), and passengers can customize their trip experience with seat selection, travelling in an extra-large seat with food and greater flexibility for a small surcharge. Premium fares apply to reserved seats in First (Confort). Passengers in the latter category have lounge access and a complimentary meal and beverage served from a food trolley pushed through the train. This class also comes

with luxurious reclining leather seats with a seat on either side of the aisle. Wi-Fi is free on this service, and this is being extended to cover all AVE services in Spain. It includes some entertainment content, such as recent films and live La Liga matches (La Liga is the familiar name for the first-division football league played in Spain). Wheelchair access and space exist on AVE trains.

Renfe also allows the option of travelling in a quiet coach, which is particularly appealing to those travelling for business and trying to complete some work during the journey. Films shown on roof-mounted screens are also offered, with the audio provided by headsets that are handed out by the crew.

Left High-speed trains operated by Renfe are known as 'Pato', which means duck and refers to the duckbill shape of the front of the locomotive.

Opposite Avlo is a high-speed train service operated by Renfe with the highest passenger capacity of 438 seats per train, 20 per cent more seats than 112 series trains (new 106 series trains will have a capacity 581 seats per train).

AL ANDALUS TRAIN

The Al Andalus Train offers a multi-day trip on a luxurious heritage train across Andalusia. Passengers travel in beautifully restored heritage carriages dating back to the 1920s. Two seven-day itineraries are offered, taking in the main tourist attractions in Seville, Málaga, Cadiz, Jerez, Ronda, Córdoba, Ubeda, Baeza and Granada. Most of these destinations are accessible via the train, while guided tours to some are done on a luxurious coach. All-inclusive packages (accommodation, meals with wine, off-train coach excursions, entrance fees and tour guides in all locations) are possible for this multi-day train touring holiday.

The train, comprising 14 carriages (two restaurants, kitchen car, bar car, lounge car, seven sleeping cars, crew car and generator car), is the longest in the country at 450 m (1,476 ft). Its 74 passengers are given a choice of two types of air-conditioned compartment: Grand Class and Deluxe Suites. The former, measuring 8.8 m² (86 ft²), is fitted out with a wardrobe, safe, luggage storage, minibar and attached bathroom. The suites of 9.9 m² (106.6 ft²) feature a double bed, which is set up by the crew each evening by converting the bench seating into a bed. Room service is available around the clock.

Other luxury multi-day trains that operate in Spain include *Costa Verde Express* (six days, Santiago de Compostela), *Transcantábrico Gran Lujo Train* (eight days, Santiago de Compostela to San Sebastián, and *La Robla Express* (three days, Bilbao to León).

BARCELONA TO MONTSERRAT

TREN CREMALLERA DE MONTSERRAT

This exciting journey begins in Barcelona before heading north-west to Manresa, situated on the Llobregat to Anoia Line. Here, passengers change on to the mountain railway line for Monistrol de Montserrat. Pilgrims travel here to worship in the basilica at the Sanctuary of the Virgin Mary, with its ancient wooden statue of the Virgin and Child that dates back over 1,000 years. Work on the adjoining monastery began in 1755. Gothic and Renaissance architectural details feature in both.

In the late nineteenth century, the need to improve access for worshippers and pilgrims arose. The opening of Monistrol de Montserrat Station on the Ferrocarrils del Nord broad-gauge railway provided an essential link to the base of the mountain. From here, worshippers travelled by road up to the monastery. In 1881, the Ferrocarrils de Muntanya de Grans Pendents was established to develop a rail ascent, and in 1892 the Montserrat Rack Railway opened. There are reports that Nazi SS leader Heinrich Himmler visited Montserrat in search of the Holy Grail.

The rack railway closed in 1957, after an accident. However, there was still interest in providing rail access, and a new route was surveyed, rebuilt and reopened in 2003. The new line of 5 km (3 miles), operated by Ferrocarrils de la Generalitat de Catalunya (FGC), begins at Monistrol de Montserrat Station, then crosses the Centenari Bridge and a motorway near Foradada Tunnel. At Monistrol Vila mid-station, the railway's rack section begins.

TRACK NOTES

The electrified mountain railway of 1,000 mm (3 ft 3⅜ in) gauge includes a section of conventional railway between Monistrol and the only intermediate station of Monistrol Vila. The line then becomes a rack railway that uses Abt cogwheel technology to assist the train in rising vertically 550 m (1,804 ft) at a maximum gradient of 15.6 per cent. The line is operated by six GTW low-floor electric motor coaches built in Switzerland by Stadler Rail and numbered AM1 to AM5 and A10. They are equipped for both adhesion and rack propulsion, and can each carry a maximum of 200 passengers. The line operates E4, a 1930-built electric loco-motive, transferred from the Vall de Núria Rack Railway located north of Barcelona. Trains run up to 30 km/h (18.6 mph) on the rack section and up to 45 km/h (28 mph) on the adhesion section.

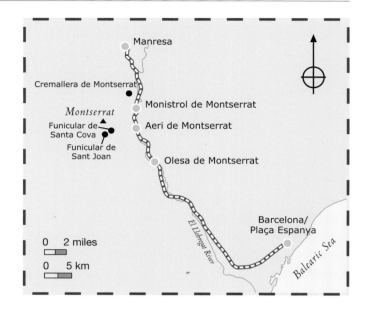

WELCOME ABOARD

The 90-minute journey departs from Barcelona's Plaça d'Espanya Station via the R5 service on FGC's Llobregat-Anoia Line. Passengers alight at Monistrol de Montserrat Station for the mountain railway. Its air-conditioned coaches have panorama windows for excellent views along the 15-minute journey. The route follows the track of the old railway, with the bulk of the journey utilizing the rack system.

The line ascends through the Àngel Tunnel, which was also used by the old railway, and crosses the new bridge at the old level crossing. Further on, the train crosses Guilleumes Bridge, where passengers can view the striking jagged rock face (in Catalan, *mont* means mount and *serrat* means serrated) before entering the Apòstols Tunnel. The train then completes the final ascent up to the Montserrat Station terminus, located just below Plaça de la Creu.

ATTENTION TO DETAIL

For those who drive, Monistrol Vila Station has a large, free parking lot with a restaurant and toilets. The Aeri de Montserrat aerial cable car presents an alternate mode of transportation to the monastery. Facilities exist on the train and at the stations for those with reduced mobility.

Trains on the rack railway depart every 20 to 35 minutes (between 8.15 a.m. and 5.15 p.m.) depending on the season, and all trains provide direct access between Monistrol Vila Station and the monastery. Traffic is heaviest in August and lightest in February.

Facilities on the mountain include accommodation, restaurants, shops, a museum and a rack railway exhibition. A daily market selling fresh local produce is staged by the villagers. The museum houses a significant archaeological exhibition and noted artworks by Caravaggio, Picasso, Monet and Dali. Audio guides and booklets are available in eight languages, including Catalan, Spanish and English. Daily performances by a boys' choir are staged except on Saturdays and holy days.

FGC also operates two funicular railways from near the rack railway summit station. The Funicular de Sant Joan heads up to the summit to offer the best panoramic bird's-eye views of the mountain and monastery.

Meanwhile, the Funicular de Santa Cova descends near the cave where, according to tradition, an image of the Virgin was discovered. This line was opened in 1929 and passed to Catalan Government Railways in 1986. It was renovated in 1991 and its original wooden-bodied cars were retained but new panoramic cars are mostly used now.

Funicular de Santa Cova provides access to a religious site at Montserrat located west of Barcelona.

SARAJEVO TO PLOČE
HEART OF THE BALKANS

The Sarajevo to Ploče rail route is a line that is 195 km (121 miles) long and runs through Bosnia and Herzegovina and the far south of coastal Croatia. The line runs from Sarajevo, the Bosnian capital, to Ploče on the Adriatic Sea. The British *Guardian* newspaper includes the Sarajevo to Mostar section of the nation's network among the world's most beautiful railways, and the country as one of the best nations to experience railway adventure. Travelling to the coast in summer was something many Sarajevans once enjoyed. International passenger services ceased a few years ago, with trains terminating at Čapljina on the Bosnian-Croatian border. Services from Čapljina to Ploče were operated by bus. However, seasonal, weekend rail services operated by the Railways of the Federation of Bosnia and Herzegovina (ŽFBH) through to Ploče in Croatia were resumed for the summer of 2022 and could be made available in subsequent years.

The Sarajevo to Ploče rail route was built in several stages, mostly during the Austro-Hungarian occupation of Bosnia (1878–1918). The Austro-Hungarian monarchy decided to construct the Southern Line in order to establish communication as quickly as possible from the interior to the coast. The first section of this 760 mm (29.9 in) gauge line, from Metković to Mostar, was opened for traffic in June 1885. Construction of the Southern Line from Mostar towards Sarajevo was continued, and in August 1888 the Mostar to Ostrožac section of the line was opened for traffic. The first train reached Konjic in November 1889. The section from Konjic to Sarajevo was opened for traffic in August 1891, which completed the connection with the Adriatic Sea. The line from Metković to Ploče was built between 1918 and 1942.

After the Second World War, the construction of standard-gauge lines and the reconstruction of the Sarajevo to Ploče line took place. It reopened in October 1968, and the line was electrified in 1969. Sections of the track were damaged during the Bosnian War (1992–1995), but have subsequently been repaired.

Speed limits, often as low as 20 km/h (12.4 mph), were in place then on sections of the track, but few complained as the route was revered for its beauty by locals and tourists. All passengers enjoyed travelling along the scenic Neretva Valley, with the river flowing through forest-covered mountains.

TRACK NOTES

Nine-car Spanish high-speed TALGO carriages hauled by 441-905 electric locomotives are used on the route. Under ideal conditions, TALGO trains can attain speeds of up to 220 km/h (137 mph), but due to the current configuration of Bosnia's rail infrastructure such speeds are currently not possible. Work is in progress to upgrade the track to enable speeds of up to 160 km/h (99 mph).

The line passes through 102 tunnels and crosses 96 bridges on its three and a half hour journey from Sarajevo to Ploče. Just beyond Sarajevo, the route becomes a single track and remains as such for most of the journey, apart from passing tracks located at most stations.

WELCOME ABOARD

The service commences in Sarajevo, situated 550 m (1,804 ft) above sea level, and terminates on the Adriatic Sea coast. The Bosnian capital is located in the Sarajevo Valley, in the middle of the Dinaric Alps. The city was founded by the Ottomans in 1461, and it has a complex history. Sarajevo became part of the Austro-Hungarian Empire in 1878. The city was etched into history when Archduke Franz Ferdinand of Austria was assassinated here in June 1914, with the incident triggering the First World War. Sarajevo station is more functional than aesthetic, with an old steam locomotive located on the platform (usually number one), from where the train to Ploče departs. The route largely follows the route of the River Neretva and passes through many tunnels. The Ivan Tunnel, which is 3.2 km (2 miles) long, is one of the first tunnels and the most significant that the train passes through.

The descent down to Konjic is spectacular as the line clings to the steep mountains, crossing numerous viaducts and passing through more tunnels. From Konjic, the railway operates quite close to the River Neretva, which is very narrow here, with the line carved into the steep folded rock. The Neretva, a large karst river (within limestone bedrock), begins its meandering journey from several glacial lakes located above Konjic in the Dinaric Alps. As such, it has been rated as the world's coldest river. The Stara Čapljina Bridge in Konjic was built in 1682–1683 and is one of Bosnia's best-preserved Ottoman bridges, rebuilt after being destroyed in the Second World War.

Jablanica Lake, between Konjic and Jablanica, is a popular destination for recreation, especially in summer. Visitors participate in swimming and watersports on the lake and hiking along trails through the surrounding forests.

The stretch of track between Jablanica and Mostar offers a picturesque array of twists and turns as the train continues to pass along the Neretva River. Jagged cliffs hem everything in from both sides of the narrow valley.

Mostar is one of the most famous parts of the journey as it is the home of the famous Stari Most (or Old Bridge), and named after the 'mostari', who were the bridge keepers. It is now recognized by UNESCO as a World Heritage Site. The original bridge was built between 1557 and 1566 by architect Harudin. Its bombing and destruction by Bosnian-Croatian artillery in November 1993

Direct trains between Sarajevo (Bosnia and Herzegovina) and Ploče (Croatia) recommenced in July 2022 after an eight-year hiatus.

Above Electric locomotives are used to haul TALGO carriages along this very scenic route.

Right A modern Spanish-designed TALGO train travelling the Neretva River on a section of the railway.

Opposite The Sarajevo to Mostar train crossing the Drežnica Bridge over Neretva River.

was broadcast on global television but contributed to peace being reached in the Balkans. Rebuilt with UNESCO funding, it reopened in 2004.

In a city with a long history, passengers should consider alighting here, spending at least a day exploring its sights and rejoining a later train. Bosnia's fifth largest city is located on the River Neretva, where the Ottomans built its famous landmark bridge in the sixteenth century. It is considered one of the country's most visited landmarks as it is an exemplary example of Islamic architecture in the Balkans.

Mostar is one of Bosnia's most fascinating cities, with some ruins dating back to the Roman era. While the iconic bridge is Mostar's most important attraction, it is not the only structure of important heritage value. Buildings such as the Bishop's Ordinariate, Halebija Towers, a Catholic Church and Franciscan Monastery, an Ottoman *hammam* or public bath, a clock tower, and several mosques, including Zaim Hadži Mehmed-bega and Karađoz Bey, built by Sinan, the famous Ottoman architect. Its Second World War Partisan Memorial Cemetery is another important symbol of the city. There are other historical sites, such as the Tekija Dervish Monastery and fortress in Blagaj, to the south-east of Mostar.

Čapljina is the last town in Bosnia and Herzegovina before reaching the Croatian border. It and the Croatian town of Metković, located just over the border, have significant commercial and other links.

Ploče is located on the Adriatic coast in Dalmatia, just north of the Neretva Delta, and is the natural seaside end point of most north–south routes through the central Dinaric Alps. This makes it the primary seaport used by Bosnia and Herzegovina. While it is more of an industrial city and port, some tourist attractions are located along the Croatian coastline. Ploče is regarded as a gateway to adventure, with activities such as kayaking and swimming at Lake Baćina, and kite surfing and biking being possibilities. A popular place to cycle is through the vineyards of the Jezero Valley, where a glass of wine is the reward for the rigorous exercise. The Makarska Riviera between Gradac and Brela offers an isolated and near-deserted coastline.

The coastal Croatian town of Makarska to the north and the popular port city of Dubrovnik to the south are both approximately 100 km (60 miles) and a two-hour drive from Ploče.

ATTENTION TO DETAIL

TALGO trains are equipped with music channels, dining cars, Wi-Fi, onboard entertainment and air conditioning. The seats (first- and second-class seating) are comfortable, and can be turned in the direction of travel. These carriages offer good views of the passing and ever-changing landscape along the route, with the left-hand side offering better views from Sarajevo to Ploče. Other facilities include toilets, accessibility for those with limited mobility, and space allocated for transporting foldable bicycles. There is a bar car on the train serving hot and cold beverages.

Some useful terms to navigate Bosnian trains include *brži voz* (fast train), *lokalni voz* (local train), *platforma* (platform) and *voz* (train).

ROMANIA
MOCĂNIȚA MARAMUREȘ

ROMANIA'S NARROW-GAUGE FORESTRY RAILWAY

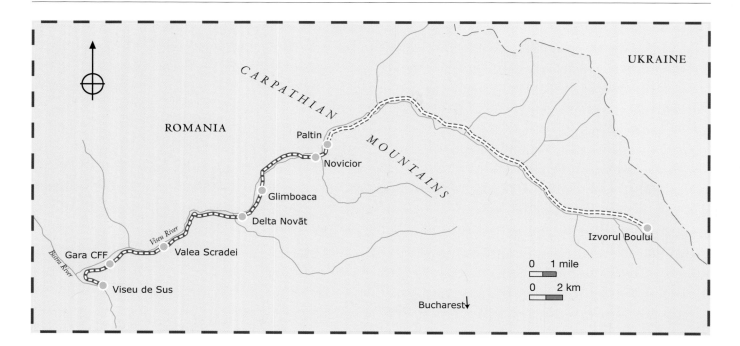

TRACK NOTES

Several wood-fired locomotives are used on the line: 764-211 (built in Austria by Krauss/Linz more than 100 years ago), 763-193 (German built), and five Romanian locos mostly built in Reșița (0-8-0T), where there is now a steam-locomotive museum. Diesel locomotives are used for logging trains, but without the impact and joy that a steam locomotive offers. Unlike standard-gauge trains in Romania that operate on a 1,435 mm (4 ft 8½ in) gauge track, the Mocănița track is a 760 mm (2 ft 5¹⁵⁄₁₆ in) track for easier access through the circuitous valley. The maximum speed is 30 km/h (18.6 mph), but trains rarely hit top gear.

WELCOME ABOARD

The train departs from Vișeu de Sus in Maramureș, just south of the border with Ukraine and some 380 km (236 miles) north of the capital, Bucharest. It takes two hours to reach Paltin – the return trip lasts six hours, with two hours allocated to experiencing Paltin's sights. The train travels slowly beside the stream and through remote villages, farms and coniferous forests, making the occasional stop to enable photography. It also stops to take on water for the boiler. It works hard as it forges its way up the

This short private railway proceeds from Vișeu de Sus to Paltin along the scenic and forested Vaser Valley in the mountainous northern Romanian region of Maramureș. It is a narrow-gauge line operated by a steam locomotive referred to as Mocănița. One suggestion for the reason for this name is that it means 'coffee machine', referring to the steam engine because its driving gear resembles an Italian-style espresso machine. Several other Mocănița routes operate in Romania, including Mocănița Transylvania. This utilitarian route was built by the state-run forestry railway CFF (Căile Ferate Forestiere) to transport logs to mills for processing, and the Maramureș route is still used as a forestry line. The locomotives that operate along this line are among some of the last in the world to run on wood fuel.

Work on the line was initiated by Casa Autonomă a Pădurilor Statului (CAPS) in 1933, and over the decades there were several branch lines. Just 45 km (28 miles) of track remain open for daily service, depending on working conditions. Regular summer and public holiday tourist trains operate on a daily basis during the season, but only to Paltin, 21.6 km (13.4 miles) along the track.

mountain through deep, forest-lined valleys dissected by a fast-f lowing river.

At Paltin, time is allocated for a forest walk along a marked trail and to eat lunch or have a picnic by the river. The locals also stage a dance performance while dressed in traditional clothing. After a two-hour break, the train makes its return run to Vişeu de Sus, laden with contented passengers and cut logs stacked on several rail wagons.

ATTENTION TO DETAIL

This popular tourist service operates from March to November, and booking well in advance online is recommended for the four trains that could operate. The first train departs at 9 a.m., and the other three leave at 30-minute intervals.

Some carriages are open, which is ideal for sightseeing and photography, but can make the carriages quite smoky. The wooden seating is rudimentary, and passengers may want to bring a small pillow along. There is limited mobile-phone connectivity beyond Vişeu de Sus. The train rattles, jerks and hisses along the line, with the left-hand side on the journey up being the best for photography. Photos are best taken on the way up the mountain as the locomotive

Rail enthusiasts can ride on Europe's last narrow-gauge forestry steam railway on its daily journey into the Carpathians to extract logs from the forests.

is repositioned at Paltin and travels backwards to Vişeu de Sus.

Groups exceeding 15 people can book or rent a full carriage, and/or the train can be chartered to continue beyond Paltin. Because it is a working train, it operates on most days, with special trips in the spring, Easter and on most public holidays. Special tickets provide seating in a closed carriage, food, beverages and a seat cushion. R. G. Holz Company, the operators, offer private charters and trains for corporate events, including two-day excursions with on-train accommodation available back at Vişeu de Sus. Trips do not always go according to plan, so passengers should be prepared to allocate much of the day just in case something untoward happens.

The closest CFR national passenger railway station is at Vişeude Jos, 4 km (2.5 miles) away, on the railway line from Sighetu Marmaţiei to Salva.

Mocăniţa is not a museum service, as timber is extracted from the forests daily except for weekends and public holidays. However, steam locomotives are used, where possible, for tourist services.

BULGARIA
SEPTEMVRI TO DOBRINISHTE

ALPINE RAILWAY IN THE BALKANS

The Septemvri to Dobrinishte single-track line is Bulgaria's only operational 760 mm (2 ft 5¹⁵⁄₁₆ in), narrow-gauge railway. Operated by Bulgarian State Railways (BDŽ), it offers four daily passenger trains, with the journey taking five hours. The line, which is 125 km (78 miles) long, passes through spectacular gorges and river valleys along the way and adopts demanding railway engineering to negotiate the often steep track.

The decision was made in 1920 to build the narrow-gauge railway from Sarambey (Septemvri) to Nevrokop (Gotse Delchev). The railway was built in several stages in 1921–1945 over a total length of 125 km (78 miles), but the line only reached Dobrinishte. The original plan to continue to Gotse Delchev was never realized. A few branch lines were also opened, but these have since closed. Progress was slow, and the work was mostly done manually. The railway was used to exploit resources such as timber and coal, as well as to carry passengers.

The route proceeds from Septemvri on the main line from Sofia to Ihtiman, Plovdiv and Dobrinishte Line, passing through the towns of Velingrad, Yakoruda, Razlog, Bansko and Dobrinishte. The line links the western part of the Upper Thracian Plain with the Western Rhodopes, Rila and Pirin Mountains. It is often referred to as the Alpine railway in the Balkans.

TRACK NOTES

Some eight locomotives, dating back to 1949 (Number 60976), are maintained by the railway. However, locomotive 60976 is the only steam locomotive in working condition, and it is used for tourist trains. In the 1960s and '70s, heavy traffic along the line (more than 10 passenger, freight and mixed services per day) saw the introduction of 10 Henschel AG (Germany) diesel locomotives. These Class 75 engines are still in service. Some Class 77 locomotives also work the line. Trains travel at a maximum speed of 50 km/h (31 mph), which is perfect for admiring the ever-changing scenery and the 25 stations.

WELCOME ABOARD

This first section of 39 km (24 miles) starts at Septemvri, which is the junction for the standard-gauge line from Sofia to Plovdiv. The train has a toilet, but passengers are advised to bring their

own food and beverages as these are not available on the train. The first stop is at Varvara Station, which was the former junction for the Pazardzhik branch line. Here, the line crosses the River Chepinska via an iron bridge. The train travels along the picturesque gorge and through Marko Nikolov and Tsepina. Some of the level crossings along the route are manually operated.

The train starts climbing towards Kostandovo on a slope that is 32 per cent in parts. After passing the station, the line descends into the Velingrad Valley. There are 10 tunnels between Marko Nikolov and Dolene, and the open track between some tunnels is covered to prevent damage from falling rocks.

The section between Velingrad and Yakoruda is the most demanding and includes four spirals, 25 tunnels and a high pass. The line begins to climb from the River Ablanitsa, heading towards Ostrets and Tsvetino. After Tsvetino, the line passes through the Lyuta Reka River Valley to reach Sveta Petka. The train climbs 224 m (800.5 ft) over the next 10 km (6.2 miles). The line crosses a stone arch bridge and negotiates 16 tunnels, along two spirals and one 180-degree turn. The line passes under itself two times in tunnels 18 and 24. In this section, the train changes direction six times at an average incline of 30 per cent. The climbing ends

at Avramovo Station after tunnel 32, which is 314 m (1.030 ft) long. At an altitude of 1,267m (4,157 ft), the railway station is the highest in the Balkans.

After Avramovo, the route is a steep, long descent through the valley of the River Dreshtenets. After Smolevo Station, the train turns on to a third spiral to pass under itself in tunnel 34. Soon after there is a fourth spiral and the last tunnel on the line. The train stops at Yakoruda for passengers who want to visit its mineral baths and admire its beautiful nature.

After stopping at Yurukovo and Dagonovo, the railway passes Belitsa and General Kovachev. The line then leaves the Mesta River valley to head along the smaller valley of the River Iztok. The train stops at a few more stations before reaching its Dobrinishte terminus. In winter, many passengers use the mineral spas here or head off to the nearby skiing resort of Bansko.

The passenger train operated by Bulgarian State Railways (BDŽ) from Septemvri to Dobrinishte is the only narrow-gauge line still operating in the country. The picturesque journey through the valleys and gorges between Rila, Pirin and Rhodopes takes five hours along what is often referred to as the alpine railway in the Balkans.

ATTENTION TO DETAIL

Passenger services only operate along the line, with four trains per day in each direction. Trains depart Septemvri for Dobrinishte at 2.20 a.m., 8.50 a.m., 12.40 p.m. and 4.10 p.m., while trains in the other direction depart Dobrinishte at 6.25 a.m., 10.25 a.m., 2.40 p.m. and 6.05 p.m. Rail tickets for this journey and others in the country can be purchased directly from the Bulgarian State Railways (BDŽ) website.

RESOURCES

USEFUL CONTACTS

Austrian Federal Railway (¯OBB) www.oebb.at
Azienda Regionale Sarda Trasporti (ARST) www.arst.sardegna.it
Bayerische Zugspitzbahn Bergbahn www.zugspitze.de
Bernese Oberland Railway www.jungfrau.ch
Bernina Express www.rhb.ch
Bulgarian State Railways (BDŽ) www.bdz.bg
Centovalli Railway www.centovalli.ch
Chemins de Fer de la Corse (CFC) www.cf-corse.corsica
Comboios de Portugal (CP) www.cp.pt
Dampfbahn Furka-Bergstrecke (DFB) www.dfb.ch
Eurostar www.eurostar.com
FarRail Tours www.farrail.com
Ferrocarrils de la Generalitat de Catalunya (FGC) www.fgc.cat
Friends of West Highland Lines www.westhighlandline.org.uk
Giant's Causeway & Bushmills Railway
  www.giantscausewayrailway.webs.com
Glacier Express www.glacierexpress.ch
Harzer Schmalspurbahnen www.hsb-wr.de
Inlandsbanan, The www.inlandsbanan.se
Jungfrau Railways www.jungfrau.ch
Keith and Dufftown Railway www.keith-dufftown-railway.co.uk
Man in Seat 61 www.seat61.com
Matterhorn Gotthard Bahn www.matterhorngotthardbahn.ch
Nordic Visitor www.nordicvisitor.com
North Yorkshire Moors Railway www.nymr.co.uk
Northern Ireland Railways www.translink.co.uk
Pinzgau Local Railway www.pinzgauerlokalbahn.at
Railways of the Federation of Bosnia and Herzegovina (ŽFBH)
  www.zfbh.ba
Renfe www.renfe.com
Rhaetian Railway www.rhb.ch
Semmering Railway www.semmeringbahn.at
Semmering Tourist Bureau www.semmering.at
Severn Valley Railway www.svk.co.uk
Slovakian Railway Company www.zssk.sk
SNCF www.sncf-connect.com
Snowdon Mountain Railway www.snowdonrailway.co.uk
Strathspey Railway www.strathspeyrailway.co.uk
Swedish Railway (SJ) www.sj.se
Swiss Federal Railways (SBB) www.sbb.ch
Swiss Travel System www.SwissTravelSystem.com
Trenitalia www.italiatren.com
Trenino Verde www.treninoverde.com
Venice Simplon Orient Express www.belmond.com
Visit Norway www.visitnorway.com
Vy (Norway) www.nsb.no.
Westbahn www.westbahn.at

FURTHER READING

Bowden, D. 2020. *Great Railway Journeys in Australia and New Zealand*. John Beaufoy Publishing.
Bowden, D. 2022. *Great Railway Journeys in Asia*. John Beaufoy Publishing.
Bryson, B. 1991. *Neither Here Nor There, Travels in Europe*. Secker and Warburg.
Bryson, B. 2015. *The Road to Little Dribbling – More Notes from a Small Island*. Penguin Random House.
Christie, Agatha. 1934. *Murder on the Orient Express*. Collins.
Palin, Michael. 2007. *New Europe*. Weidenfeld and Nicholson.
Solomon, B. 2015. *The World's Most Exotic Railway Journeys*. John Beaufoy Publishing.
Solomon, B. 2020. *The World's Great Rail Journeys*. John Beaufoy Publishing.
Theroux, P. 1975. *The Great Railway Bazaar by Train through Asia*. Hamish Hamilton.
Theroux, P. 1990. *Travelling the World*. Sinclair-Stevenson Ltd.
Theroux, P. 2008. *Ghost Train to the Eastern Star*. Houghton Mifflin.

ACKNOWLEDGEMENTS

Many people contributed valuable knowledge, photos, insights and feedback in compiling this book. Particular thanks are extended to Heide Baumgärtner (Harzer Schmalspurbahnen), Ivan Bellais (SNCF), Andrea Beran (Semmering Tourist Bureau), Tamara Boscia (Embassy of Italy, Kuala Lumpur), Lesley Carr (SVR), Doug Carmichael, David Crossley, Bruce Crowe and Alan Moir (Keith and Dufftown Railway), Fraser McDonald (Friends of West Highland Lines), Anne Dallaporta (Marseille Tourism), Rosa Gomes (CP), Jessie den Harder (Glacier Express), Carrie Druce (Snowden Mountain Railway), Volker Emersleben (Deutsche Bahn), Therese Fanqvist (Inlandsbanan), Peter Fisher (NYMR), Lilly Freudmayer (Austrian National Tourist Office), Monica Sanchez Gonzalez (Tourist Office of Spain), Kerry Graye (Translink), Cécile Gruffat (Chamonix Mont Blanc), Kait Yeen Lai (Spain), Remo Käser (Jungfrau Railways), Helen Lumb, Bernd Seiler, Mihaela Berteanu, Doug Williams (Močanița, Romania), Alexandra Mackintosh (Visit Lake District), Joëlle Martin, Paul Smit (Tourist Office Menton), Paola Mascia (ARST), Françoise Mélard-Peretti (Corsica Tourism Agency), Fred Matthews, Sini Mesilaakso (VR Finland), Jonas Olsson (SJ Swedish Railways), Ellis Pettigrew (Serco), Robert Rhys and Rob Cowley (Cumbria Tourism), Wiebke Rummel (Siemens Mobility), Ana Maria de Carvalho Santos (CP), Dieter Scharf (Austrian National Tourist Office), Anna Serret (FGC), Dan Shorthouse (SVR), Vlado Soldo, Sejdalija Kešetovíc, Senka Radic (ŽFBH), Mesilaakso Sinihannele (VR), Brian Solomon, Dominika Štefková (High Tatras Tourism Association), Ingrid Thomson (Glamis Castle), Kristian Vaklinov (BDZ), Filipina Viera (Associação de Turismo do Porto e Norte, AR) and Rudy Wiranto (Swiss Travel System).

INDEX

NOTE This index is divided into two parts – Countries & Regions and Train Journeys.

First published in the United Kingdom in 2023 by John Beaufoy Publishing,
11 Blenheim Court, 316 Woodstock Road, Oxford OX2 7NS, England
www.johnbeaufoy.com

10 9 8 7 6 5 4 3 2 1

ISBN 978-1-913679-52-1

Design by Ginny Zeal
Editing and index by Krystyna Mayer
Cartography by William Smuts
Project management by Rosemary Wilkinson

Printed and bound in Malaysia by Times Offset (M) Sdn. Bhd.

Photograph credits
All photos by David Bowden except:
Fredrik Ahlsen (p.65), ARST SpA (p.131), Austrian Tourism (p.115), Bayerische Zugspitzbahn (p.109), Belmond (p.17, p.18, p.19, p.35, p.36 top and bottom), David Bisset (p.50), Bulgarian State Railways (p.155), Anthony Carwithen (p.48), Cinque Terre (p.127, p.128, p.129), Comboios de Portugal (p.139, p.140 top and bottom), Maxime Coquard (p.61), Corsica Tourism Agency (p.63), Bruce Crowe (p. 37), Bon Crowley (p.42, p.43), Deutsche Bahn (p.100, p.101, p.102 top and bottom), Eurostar (p.23 bottom), Therese Fanqvist (p.5, p.69), Matthias Fend - Bayerische Zugspitzbahn (p.108, p.110, p.111 left and right), Ferrovia Vigezzina-Centovalli (p.98, p.99), Giant's Causeway & Bushmills Railway (p.29), Jason Hood (p.49), Hungarian National Railway (p.11), Inlandsbanan (p.70), Sejdalija Kešetović (p.151), Pekka Keskinen (p.75, p.77 top and bottom), Lucy Knott (p.30), Erich Kodym (p.118 top), Helen Lumb (p.153), Lucy Maddox (p.51), Mariazellerbahn (p.113), Marriott Hotels & Resorts (p.23 top), Micalef OTCM (p.59), Leif Johnny Olestad - Visit Norway (p.66), Guido Pijper (p.7 top), Plan International Laos (p.141), Stephan Ray (p.8), Renfe (p.12, p.13, p.142, p.143, p.144, p.145 top and bottom), Valerio Santos (p.136), Christel Sasso - Alstrom (p.133), Volker Schadach (p.105, p.106, p.107), Horst Schöttner (p.117, p.119), ScotRail (p.53, p.54), SNCF (p.58), Shutterstock/Sergii Figurnyi (p.135 top) and Lucamoto (p.135 bottom), Siemens Mobility (p.9), Sandy Smeaton (p.55), Paul Smit (p.125), Snowdon Railway (p.45, 46 top and bottom), Brian Solomon (p.15, p.16, p.20, p.21, p.74), Spanish Tourism (p.147), Dominika Stefkova (p.122, p.123), Swiss Travel System (p.60, p.79, p.80, p.82, p.83 bottom, p.85, p.86, p.87, p.89 top, p. 97), Derek Thompson (p.31 top and bottom, p.32, p.33), Gordon Tosbell (p.39), Tourism Norway (p. 67), Translink (p.27, p.28), Visit Finland (p.73, p.94 top, p.76), Visit Lake District (p.41), Vlado Soldo (p.149, p.150 top and bottom), Håkan Wike (p.71), Kevin Winter (p.38), Franz Zwickl - Vienna Alps (p118 bottom).